Michele Hanson has created a  fe in her famous weekly *Guardian* col <s>_____</s> years she has chronicled the teenage years of her daughter, Treasure, and the final years of her mother. *Treasure: the Trials of a Teenage Terror*, *What Treasure Did Next*, and *The Age of Dissent*, based on the *Guardian* columns, were published by Virago, serialised on Radio 4 and made into a BBC cartoon series. Michele regularly appears on radio and TV, most recently as one of the Grumpy Old Women. She lives in north London, these days mostly on her own with her two boxer dogs. She is delighted with solitude.

Clarice, aged 35, during the Second World War.
She was pregnant with me at the time.

LIVING WITH MOTHER

MOTHER

Right to the Very End

MICHELE HANSON

Virago

VIRAGO

First published in Great Britain in 2006 by Virago Press in association with
Guardian Books

Guardian Books is an imprint of Guardian Newspapers Ltd

ISBN-13: 978-1-84408-384-8
ISBN-10: 1-84408-384-5

Typeset in Spectrum by M Rules
Printed and bound in Great Britain by
Clays Ltd, St Ives plc

Virago Press
An imprint of
Little, Brown Book Group
Brettenham House
Lancaster Place
London WC2E 7EN

A member of the Hachette Livre Group of Companies

www.virago.co.uk
www.guardian.co.uk

ACKNOWLEDGEMENTS

To my mother, and to Hazel, Jacqueline, Jennifer, Dicky, Carol, Syrrel, Olga, John, Florence, Veronica, Jane, Jenny and all the other friends, relatives and carers who helped me and Amy to look after her and to make the last ten years of her life happier.

I would like to thank Clare Longrigg, my editor at the *Guardian* Women's page, for thinking that these columns would be a good idea in the first place; all the editors who let them carry on for twelve years: Sally Weale, Libby Brooks, Raekha Prasad, Esther Addley, Becky Gardiner, Emily Wilson, Clare Margetson, Laura Barton, Melissa Denes, Katherine Viner, Joanna Moorehead, and Kira Cochrane; Lucy Clouting for her invaluable help; Ruth Petrie, for thinking they ought to make a book, and Lennie Goodings at Virago, for agreeing with her.

ESCAPE FROM DEATH ROW

I have just rescued my mother from Brighton General Hospital, or the antechamber to Hell.

'Don't send her there,' I asked the doctor, the sister, the nurses and a manager. 'Her husband recently died there on a trolley, her sister-in-law developed huge and fatal bed sores. She'll think she's never coming out again.'

They sent her there.

'We have a bed crisis.' Sister rings me apologetically at ten at night from the Royal Sussex. 'We're sending her to Brighton General.'

'We call it Death Row,' I drone.

'Oh I wish you wouldn't,' says Sister prettily. 'It's not that bad.'

My mother has angina. She is very anxious, say all medical staff. The anxiety is making the angina worse. Then they send her to Death Row to relax.

I whizz down from London to get her out. It is unpleasant having an elderly parent incarcerated in such a place. She is wild to escape, dressed and striding up and down the ward waving her stick, the only patient moving. The others are very pale and mostly asleep. The odd subdued visitor sits in attendance. It is deathly quiet.

But we cannot leave. My mother's supply of pills is missing. Pharmacy cannot find them. This is obviously another ploy to minimise anxiety. Another delay. Just as we are about to leave in a bate without them and return later, the pills appear. We escape at last and whizz to the post office, the fish shop, lunch club and hairdresser. No angina. My mother rings the doctor to report her release.

'What do you want now?' snaps the receptionist. I am keen to dart round and give her a sharp slap but my mother is used to this. She is eighty-nine and has seen it all before.

1

'I have gout, fits and pains in my chest,' my father told his doctor not so long ago.

'You are eighty-three,' said the doctor in a grump. 'I'll be lucky if I live that long.' He zoomed in and out in a trice and hurried off to the next patient, and there are hundreds along the south coast, all suffering from Eighty-three, or even Seventy-three, and all the ages in between. Ill health can be a grey area for the elderly. After a certain age in Sussex and along much of the south coast and in other parts of Britain, one cannot be ill. Only old.

I think there may be a useful catch here for the health service. If one is eighty-three rather than ill, then it's social services responsibility rather than health service. Health service is free, but social service has to be paid for by the client. The health service can make enormous savings on people who are found to be seventy- or eighty-three.

My father was taken into Brighton General after a fit and lay in bed babbling temporarily. 'What's he like at home?' the nurses asked us in a concerned way. 'What's his quality of life?'

'Perfectly all right,' we said. 'He visits the betting shop daily, reads the runners, selects winners, goes to Waitrose, drives the car, reads about World War I in depth.'

'We shan't resuscitate if he arrests again,' said the nursing staff gravely. 'Quality of life,' they murmured. 'What's he normally like?' they asked again. 'We take his age and record into account.'

'He's perfectly all right,' we shouted. 'There's nothing wrong with his quality of life,' but they didn't believe us. And then they consigned him to Death Row, with a skeleton staff of angel, overworked, underpaid nurses to look after the glut of geriatrics. But perhaps management felt there was no point them doing very much. The patients were after all suffering from Eighty-Three, a hopeless condition with no known cure. My father escaped twice, confounded them, recovered his speech and his quality of life. The third time finished him off. Thank goodness we escaped. For now.

MOVING

My mother is in turmoil. She must make a horrid decision and she can't. Shall she move in here with us or shall she stay in her own lovely flat in Hove? There things are all on one level. She has two lavatories, one bidet, comfortable chairs, peace and quiet and tidiness. But she cannot spend the nights alone. All sorts of dreadful things may happen: angina, heart attacks, robbers, vertigo, nightmares, insomnia, loneliness or sudden death. These are the things she lies sweating and expecting when she sleeps alone.

But in our house she is safe. I am on hand to summon the doctor or ambulance. Unfortunately, our home is dreadful. It is full of mountainous stairs, mess, dribbling barking dog, noise, rows and the screaming Daughter and Granddaughter.

And the sofa is too low, the chairs too narrow, the stairs too many and too steep, the meals too late, the tea too weak, the whole place too messy and Gardener (my partner) and visitors irritating.

It's only a pretend choice anyway. She doesn't really have one, which throws her into a fury. She must come and live here with us in Hell. It is at least entertaining. She tries to be positive about it. And we have better services up here in town: the doctors, the dentist, the hospital and the social workers are charming. Down in Hove they tend to be curt, surly and always in a hurry, perhaps because of the glut of elderly people down there. And the social club up here is superior. There is bridge, dancing, bargain hairdressing, and the lunches are divine. Her friend there, Esther, asks her a difficult question over lunch.

'Tell me, Clarice,' she says, looking rather anxious, 'you're living with your daughter. What's it like? Because I might have to do it.'

'I told her,' says my mother, tactful as ever, 'that you do things

3

your way and I mustn't interfere. That's the way you run your life.'

This must be an edited version. But what will Esther do? What will several million other Aged Ps do but have to leave their homes and live with their children, or watch their life's savings evaporate in a trice paying for residential care?

A drear thought. We cannot bear my mother to do it. She does not want to end up sitting in a dull semi-circle of brown or green armchairs watching the telly. At least most people in our house can walk about. If we all try to scream less, put in an outside lavatory, train the dog not to dribble and bark, make nice strong tea and early dinners, things would improve no end.

Meanwhile, my friend Rosemary's mother is rather envious of my mother. She longs to move into her daughter's home. But Rosemary has the poorly husband to look after, who stays indoors reading biographies, and two children and a cat and a full-time gruelling job. This is not an easy time of life. Rosemary and I are beginning to long for retirement, when we too will be able to sit about reading large biographies. I shall send my mother over on Sunday to give Rosemary's mother the lowdown on life with a daughter, her adolescent child, dog, paramour and messy house. It will be a realistic picture. My mother is not one for toning things down. She tends to speak frankly. She has herself considered sheltered accommodation, but even for that one has to pay through the nose.

'I might as well be miserable here for free,' says my mother sensibly.

DANGEROUS ENCOUNTERS

My mother is tremendously forthright. 'I didn't know you had such fat legs,' she roars cheerily at Olga, who is wearing some new boldly patterned leggings. She doesn't really mean fat, she means not skinny, but this doesn't help Olga. She laughs bravely, although knocked sideways by this harsh critique.

I remind my mother that such personal remarks are hurtful, but she is unashamed. 'I like fat legs,' says she. 'John Cleese has got lovely legs.' She has admired them ever since *A Fish Called Wanda*. To my mother, plump is beautiful. She stares tragically at her elegant twig-like teenage granddaughter, remembering the chubbly, cuddly baby that she once was. 'You used to be such a lovely fat baby,' she moans in public. Granddaughter is mortified.

We live on a knife edge. People are being offended right, left and centre. An outing with my mother is even more fraught with danger. She will attack members of the public physically and ver-bally. The size, strength and ferocity of the victim means nothing to her. Only yesterday she chose a huge bare-chested fellow with bulging, rippling muscles and a bullet head for a telling-off.

This gentleman was strolling across the road with his three small children as we drove up it to a T-junction at a slow crawl. He flew into a fury, as if we had roared past shaving the skin off his nose and within a whisker of slaughtering his children.

'Arsehole,' he bellowed.

Naturally my mother was horrified. 'That's no way to speak in front of children,' she roared. 'You're the arsehole.'

If she had thought for one nano-second before speaking she would have realised that it is foolish to correct and speak abusively to a fellow of his stature when one is eighty-nine and when he is only two feet from your wide open car window.

He approached the window in a menacing way, growling vile threats at my mother, who argued back fiercely. I ordered her to remain silent but she refused. She rarely obeys orders, especially from her own child. Luckily a gap appeared in the traffic in the nick of time and we whizzed to safety.

'Please don't do that again,' I warned my mother. 'Do not shout at men like that. He doesn't care that you're a frail old lady. He nearly punched your head in.'

'He wouldn't dare,' she snapped boldly. 'I'd have hit him with my stick.'

What luck that we managed to escape. My mother has not realised that the nineties are a fairly brutal period when being her age and female will never save you from a punch on the nose. In fact muggers find frail old ladies rather tempting. They can steal purses from them effortlessly. One half-hearted slap and the old ladies go down like ninepins. I have warned her never to open the door when I am out and never to walk about the streets carrying her handbag.

Minutes later she realised the error of her ways. 'I should think before I open my mouth,' said she sensibly, shaking with terror at the thought of what might have happened. She only expresses such sentiments *after* a burst of kamikaze behaviour.

In this instance right was on her side. This fellow deserved a drubbing. Had I only been 6' 6", male and muscular, I too would have given him a telling-off, but even after eighty-nine years on this earth my mother has not learnt that one is not necessarily rewarded for being right. She has, however, realised that the meek shall inherit nothing at all. It is becoming more and more difficult to sort out one's morals.

SEX LATER ON

Rosemary is desperate for her own bedroom. She has found sex something of an ordeal in recent years. After twenty-five years of marriage, she would far rather join a choir, but she has her husband to consider. He would not prefer the choir. He tends to sulk horribly. So Rosemary has struggled on. She would map out Sainsbury's on the ceiling, starting in the fruit and veg area, then through dairy products and all round, and by the time she got to soft drinks and the check-out, she'd have a trolley full and it would all be over. Husband never knew about the map.

But this week Rosemary has had enough. 'I've told him,' says she, 'that that part of our life together is over.' She looks thrilled. The husband is monosyllabic but Rosemary is determined to stick with it. She feels that at our age, a choir is more fitting. And she has her mother and her children to look after, and the sulking husband. She needs to do something pleasant with her spare time, spiritual rather than physical. At her age, fifty-six, she has rather given up on sex. It seems to be a slightly ridiculous and troublesome pastime which luckily fades out in later middle age.

But not for all of us. My mother has just spent a week down in her seaside home with a friend, tidying and throwing out rubbish. While tidying they chatted about this and that and up came the topic of sex. My mother is eighty-nine and has rather forgotten about this topic, but her friend hasn't.

In fact she is tremendously keen on it and has a boyfriend. At seventy-nine. My mother returns with a startling report. Not only does her friend have a sex life and speaks of it rather boldly, but she also told my mother that recently it had not been up to the desired standard. She was not having orgasms.

'She has a boyfriend,' says my mother, shocked to the core, 'and she wants orgasms as well?'

The friend has had the effrontery to go to the doctor and complain. She wants things put right. The orgasms are a must. Luckily some medicament that she was taking had been causing the problem. It was changed and the thrilling sex life resumed.

I tell my mother that nowadays women may go to the doctor and ask such things. If they dare. I must say I rather admire this lady. Demanding such rights at her age, or at any age, is a courageous step, even hidden away in the doctor's surgery. To tell a relatively new friend or any acquaintance, when one is elderly and on the chubby side, is even bolder.

Being rather staggered by her friend's revelations, my mother didn't like to ask too many questions, but she did manage one. 'Doesn't he mind all this?' she asked, pointing to the friend's podgiest area.

'He loves it,' said the friend, in a carefree way. This must be a liberated woman — sexually uninhibited, no weight problems. For thirty years my mother has battled against excess fat, and here is a woman, far chubbier than her, who couldn't give a fig. How has she done it?

At Art School, when I was only seventeen, we had a rather swizzy painting teacher, possibly in his fifties, who tried to broaden our education a little by introducing some literature and a dash of his own philosophy. He read out D.H. Lawrence in dialect (an embarrassing experience for us), and told us that 'sex was an Art and improved with practice'. Naturally we thought him a dreadful show-off. But perhaps he was spot on. My mother's friend is having the time of her life. Heaven knows what might happen to Rosemary in the choir.

REMOVALS

Selling one's home at any age is fairly grim. At eighty-nine it is a nightmare. My mother is finally relinquishing her own flat in Hove, a dangerous event. The shock of it, I have heard, can knock the elderly for six. Forced to leave their homes along the A1 (blighted by the threat of a motorway), they have been dropping like flies.

Naturally my mother is in a frenzy. She cannot sleep a wink and when awake she lives and breathes Inventory. When approached by any person at any time of the day or night she will spout lists of furnishings, fittings and contents, what's to be left, what's coming here, and wherever are we to put it?

'Do you want the soufflé dishes?' she asks, 'I'm not leaving them.' Or the favourite armchair and sofa and candlesticks and mirror. 'And what about the white plates/plants/Magimix/carving knives?' She cannot bear to leave even the tiniest scrap of property behind.

It is a nerve-wracking business. Will the buyer change her mind? She is desperately trying to beat down the price. Wait till she hears of the gargantuan charges incurred for services and repairs to the buildings. Managing Agent has obviously hired the Royal Master Craftsmen to paint the front windows.

I urge my mother not to get excited. But she is easily excited: by the dog slobbering, us leaving the lights on, the price of cheese, the relentless sound of the Hoover. Meanwhile, upstairs, her teenage granddaughter is swooning with suspected glandular fever. Our home is swirling with germs and tension.

Rosemary next door comes in for a brief visit when we are all at dinner. Rosemary joins us for some apple pie and cream and high-octane Inventory. Naturally, because of the tension, we are all roaring and shouting. Rosemary stays fifteen minutes and retires

9

shell-shocked to the safety of her own home without even finishing her pudding. She had previously thought her home rather drab and dismal, but she now sees that it is a haven of peace and culture. Its shelves of books and bits of muted but tasteful carpet and ornament make a pleasant change from our house.

Mrs X, the buyer, rings. She has reduced her offer by several thousand. My mother is stunned. We reject Mrs X's rather saucy offer. She rings back days later with a higher one. This is playing havoc with my mother's angina. Her nerves are in shreds. She longed for a peaceful old age and is not getting one. Here is her beloved home being tossed up and down on the market like a bit of old bric-a-brac. And once it is sold she has burnt her boats. She will be stuck here for ever with us.

There is nothing for it but to dress up our living room like my mother's ex-flat. Then she can pretend she's still partially there. If we can cram as much as possible into here, she will hardly realise she has moved.

Our living room is soon a replica of the Hove apartment. Not just a few items, but everything is now crammed in. We have china teacups and chandeliers and the gramophone throbs with rhumba and paso doble. We have the big mirror with ornate gold-twirling surround, ancestral portraits and my mother's flower paintings on all walls. The ground floor is a Hove simulator.

Visitors are prone to culture shock, but my mother has perked up tremendously. She lies on her own sofa wrapped in shawls and a rather glamorous turban, eating choc truffles, drinking piña colada and singing, 'Ours is a nice house ours is, it's got no rats and mouses.'

This is fairly close to a compliment.

EXTRAVAGANCE

Now that my mother lives on the premises she is able to observe the details of our life — a shocking thing to watch when one is eighty-nine. She is horrified by our expenditure. I have taken to lying about the cost of everything. I halve it. My mother is still outraged. There she is busy saving paper bags, Christmas cards and bits of string, then out I go and fritter money on a ready-made, steamed syrup pudding.

'How much was that?' she snaps, astounded by the price. 'What did you do that for?' she roars. 'I can make one.' She stamps off to the kitchen and whips one up for tuppence.

We now buy no shop cakes or biscuits. We save egg boxes, jam jars, used stamps and old sheets. We darn clothes, reuse tea bags and save rainwater. The house is filling with ancient scraps and rags. And we are not allowed to waste a crumb of food.

'It's from living through the war,' explains Rosemary. She has a touch of it herself, often running about the house turning the lights out after everyone.

'Blackout, blackout,' shouts her son in a mocking way. Soon my mother will be issuing ration books to curb our somewhat profligate lifestyle. Microwave dinners, bought puddings and oven chips will be strictly limited.

My cousin in the north is under similar constraints. Her mother (my auntie) also moans on about cost. Like me, Cousin lies and halves the cost of everything. Only last week she bought Auntie some smoked salmon for a treat. Auntie commands her to shop around, but what with a full-time job and everbody's shopping to do, she hasn't the time, so as usual she halved the price.

Naturally Auntie was thrilled with the price of the salmon. She thought it such a bargain that she gave it to the cleaning lady for a present. Cousin was furious. She now has to go shopping for more salmon and tell more lies. She and I are both enmeshed in a web of deceit.

And of course I have lied like billy-o about the stairlift. It arrived today, three hours late. My mother lies in bed glaring at the installers. She has never wanted it. 'I'm not a cripple,' she has shouted repeatedly. 'It's a bloody waste of money.'

I remind her that this is a recycled stairlift, second hand, and the minute she drops dead (we have given up on euphemisms), we will sell it and get our money back. This makes her feel better. She stops snarling at the installers. For hours they fiddle about on the stairs and I must leave them there and go to work. They are under oath not to mention cost.

But I forget my keys. What luck that my mother can now answer the door. I look through the letter box. There she is sailing downstairs on her lift. 'Ground floor, men's wear, ladies' shoes, lighting,' she calls out gaily over the grinding roar of the machinery. We are thrilled to bits, even though the lift resembles a sliding plastic lavatory and does nothing for our hallway.

My mother swans up to the lavatory on it, down again to make marmalade, up again for a rest, and down again for *Coronation Street*. She even stops mentioning the price. Encouraged by this development, Rosemary and I take her to Marks & Spencer for a new nightie. Every nightie is pink or cream. My mother is sickened. 'I'll look like an old woman,' she shouts. She had hoped for something more dashing – in bold colours and patterns and no teeny pink flowers.

I buy myself a brassiere and halve the price. The woman behind us in the queue hears Rosemary and I discussing my mother's attitude to spending. She joins in. Her mother will buy nothing new and lives in worn and tattered rags. 'I'll make do,' says the mother heroically. 'This will last me out.'

Comparatively my mother is a spendthrift.

HAIR CRISIS

My friend Olga is having a slight hair crisis. Being an artist she has never been one for convention, but now, at fifty, she feels that some sort of style change is in order. She has felt this for months. Meanwhile her hair has looked quite wild and begun to disturb my mother. She cannot understand Olga's delay or crisis. To her the solution is simple – a cut, rinse and set is in order.

'Why doesn't she do something with her hair,' my mother moans persistently. 'It looks terrible.' She has asked Olga this same question repeatedly, but Olga does nothing. She is paralysed by indecision and as time goes on her fringe grows longer and my mother becomes more agitated. Olga's visits to our house are nerve-wracking. Will my mother say something untoward?

Forgetting that her critic is in residence, Olga rashly calls round for coffee. I have warned my mother strictly not to comment but the thought of Olga's hair has tormented her all week. She knows that women of our age may not walk about looking unkempt. For months she has racked her brains for a solution and now she has found one. She is busting to speak.

'I've been worrying about you for days,' she says to Olga, 'and today I had a good idea.'

'What is it?'

'Well, I know you don't like spending time on your hair, so why don't you buy a wig? You can get some lovely ones.' She is thrilled with her solution. Olga laughs bravely. I reprimand my mother. She is unrepentant. 'Next to *her*,' she says ruthlessly when Olga is gone, '*you* look glamorous.'

We have a yawning generation gap here which opened in my youth in the sixties and will never close. My hairstyle and mode of dress have always rather disappointed my mother and Olga's is far more outlandish. And my mother is bolder than me. Even now, on the downhill slope to death, she still refuses to tone it down.

But I shall always think fondly of Olga's hairstyle — it is similar to mine — thin, weedy, uncontrollable and bound to distress a neatly coiffed mother. I remember it at a depressing antenatal lecture that Olga and I attended in earlier middle age. I arrived first. All around sat neatly dressed couples and I sat alone with my hair in a mess. Then suddenly in burst Olga in a cloud of pottery dust with her hair in chaos. At last an ally for me in this hellhole.

'I want you to make friends with your vagina,' said the lady speaker in a forthright way.

Olga and I weren't sure that we wanted to do that. We both left the lecture quick as a flash and jumped on to a bus, screaming — two elderly primagravidas without proper hairstyles. But now sixteen years have gone by, our children have grown up and we must get ourselves in order. Our hair is now almost universally disapproved of. People will not tolerate it. Luckily for her, Olga's child is a boy, but mine is a girl who longs for a chic mother. I do my best, have the hair cut regularly, dye it reddish-purple, apply mousse after washing to give it body. People smile politely at it.

Olga and I did recently find one admirer, however. We were at a party with another witch-like friend with an outrageous pink coiffure. We had made an effort, put on our best frocks, but our hair still lacked control. A strange, bald young man in a black cloak approached us. He was full of admiration.

'It's wonderful to see women of your age with character,' said he. It almost sent us all off for a neat cut and set.

MAD ON COOKING

My mother is dead keen on cooking. It helps her to relax and has brought her a new role in life – chief chef to the household and teacher of haute cuisine. My friends are flooding round here to attend master classes in the kitchen. They do as they are told, listen carefully and then eat up the thrilling results. Rosemary and Olga are particularly dedicated pupils, forever copying out recipes, obeying orders and oohing and aahing.

'I forget everything else when I'm cooking,' cries my mother cheerily, whirling about the kitchen like a tornado, surrounded by admirers.

I do not attend these lessons. I have never been keen on doing as my mother tells me and somehow cannot start now. I notice that my daughter is following my example to the letter. She will not listen to the tiniest instruction, avoids all domestic tasks, but is highly skilled at microwaving. We are both a disappointment to my mother. What luck that she is encouraged and supported by my friends, and now by the telly, suddenly jam-packed with cookery programmes. She awakes every day to a new one.

'It's Kevin,' she calls happily. 'It's Delia/It's Paul and Jean. Look.' Caught up in the welter of programmes, her table is piled high with scribbled recipes and notepads and we have a thrilling menu – apple tatin, creamed celeriac, chicken with apicots, pear frangipane tart, coulis of this and that.

My mother quotes the words of famous cooks. 'Give me some rocket and balsamic vinegar and I'm anyone's,' she roars. She has made an enormous culture leap – from working-class Barrow-in-Furness, via Hove, to trendy north London. This is something of an accomplishment at her age.

15

Sadly my loathing of cooking never wavers. The more programmes, master classes, demonstrations and discussions, the worse it gets. And now we have found a new fish shop. My mother is in paradise. The fish is heavenly and cheap. It is even better than the fish in Hove. She does bulk buying. We must now be forever talking about the buying and preparation of food, especially fish.

And she has mobilised the neighbourhood. Everyone must collect windfalls, blackberries, green tomatoes and the sour cherries from next door. The fridge and freezer are bursting with pies, purées, chutneys and stewed fruits.

I must admit that on Friday my mother made the best blackberry pie on earth. Then tragedy struck. She could not eat a crumb of it. She was so exhausted and sickened by her huge bout of cooking that she could only lie weak, pale and nauseated in front of the telly sipping fizzy lemonade, a shadow of her kitchen self. It was two days before she could stomach the pie, and by then it had lost its brilliance.

'It's only nice if someone else cooks it,' my mother moaned in a heart-rending way. I agree absolutely. Today we had cheese on toast, made in a flash by me. My mother loved it.

PLAGUE WEEK

This has been plague week in our house. I have been sick, my daughter has been sick, the chap I went out to dinner with has been sick and the dog has been sick. This was a nightmare for my mother, with her bedroom right next to the bathroom. She was wakened at 3 a.m. by vile roaring noises and pitiful moans, which went on until lunchtime.

It is worrying when your primary carer is flat out on the bathroom floor or in bed semi-conscious. And our helpful neighbour Rosemary was away on holiday *and* it was bank holiday.

Then my mother was struck down. Her right eye began to hurt like billy-o and went blind. 'Get her to the eye hospital at once,' said the doctor over the phone, 'if you want to save the sight in that eye.' Luckily Olga was able to whizz my mother to hospital in her car.

But what if the eye could not be repaired? What if the other eye packed up as well? What would my mother do, unable to read, watch telly or look at the flowers? These were my horrid thoughts as I lay weakly in bed. I imagined my mother groping her way round the house, tripping over the dog and other piles of mess. I would be forever tidying and my mother would have to learn to love Radio 4 and live without watching *Coronation Street*.

Luckily none of this happened. Olga and she were back in a trice with eye drops, but imagine the flap in our house. My mother wished to contact social services at once. This had set her panicking about the future. What if I am ill again? She needs an assistant to call on when I malfunction.

I ring social services again. They heard of us months ago when we were all healthy and have already allocated us someone. She will ring tomorrow. She phones while I am out for ten minutes walking the dog. How did my mother not hear? She was clutching the new cordless phone, bought for just such emergencies. I ring back but Social Worker is now away for a few days.

My mother is ninety next week. Will she live to meet the social worker? I hear from Rosemary, who is a member of this profession, that people have been known to die waiting. Their file has been labelled 'dormant' or 'inactive', and left resting while other more critical clients are being dealt with. Sometimes the 'dormant' person fades away unnoticed.

But I am being unjust after a difficult week. The population is getting bigger, madder and sicker and social services are overworked and desperate, yet despite all this they have flooded round to our house and fixed lavatory seats, wall rails, meals on wheels and mobile library. And within days someone else appears to assess my mother's needs, which have increased.

I can tell her what they are, easy: a new, immaculately tidy ground-floor apartment with bidet, relays of polite and high-quality bridge players, a handsome, rich and charming husband for me, and most of all, a new body for herself. Meanwhile, we may have a personal care assistant twice a week.

I hear there's a bit of a waiting list.

CLEANING LADY

For months my mother has been nagging for a cleaning lady. She cannot physically do the cleaning herself, my cleaning is substandard, and my mother, feeling that she lives in a mire of filth, is sinking into gloom. She likes a gleaming tidy home, kept in order by a cleaning lady, who preferably works like a demon and never takes tea breaks. She is a ruthless employer.

Naturally I am not keen to have a cleaning lady. I feel that I will be committing an innocent person to hours of labour in a slave galley with my mother as harsh overseer, just because of my own sluttishness and inadequacies. Furthermore, slave wages will be paid as my mother is not au fait with the idea of a minimum wage and doesn't give a fig for socialist values or the new wave of middle-class guilt.

But she is determined. If I won't get a cleaning lady, then she will. As I push her along in the dread wheelchair she calls out loudly to all the local shopkeepers, 'DO YOU KNOW A CLEANING LADY?' She describes her misfortune at having to live in a slum and begs movingly for help.

Now at last she has got lucky. The greengrocer knows one. Kathy. In fact she has just passed by. She is at this very moment in the next-door launderette. He rushes off to find her. Imagine the excitement. My mother is thrilled to bits. Her life in the rubbish tip is almost over. Her saviour is only seconds away.

Soon Kathy appears. A brief interview is conducted on the pavement. She will come to look at our house later this evening. But will she want to work there? Should I quickly whirl round cleaning, polishing and tidying things up? Will she enter, shout 'Aaargh' and run away, rejecting my home as a workplace and leaving my mother in Hades?

Were my mother not present I would tend to go for casual time-keeping, long tea breaks and chats about personal lives. I have had a cleaning lady in the past, but her private life was so gripping, mine such a mess and she and I in such a state that the tea breaks rather dominated things. Her husband was a batterer, her daughter captured by Yardies, and she in need of secret lifts to meet her lover, who would wait a few streets away. Then I had my relationship with a mendacious two-timing fellow to drone on about. Every week we had another thrilling instalment. We had scarcely a moment left for work.

My mother would never have allowed things to slide like that. She carries out inspections and issues strict instructions without the weeniest twinge of guilt. She was born to rule.

What luck that Kathy and my mother fall for each other at first sight. My mother arises from her gloom-induced lethargy. They whizz about chatting, tidying and having the odd rapid slurp of tea on the wing. Meanwhile I can sit in my room undisturbed, drowning in mess, racking the empty brain or fiddling away with another useless bit of prose. We are all happy at last. More or less.

BIRTHDAYS

Last week my mother was ninety. She woke up suicidal. How can one be merry with a hernia, a gammy leg and piles? She dragged herself to the bathroom. There in the mirror was a wrinkled face surrounded by wisps of grey hair. My mother moaned in a heart-rending way and staggered back to bed.

People kept ringing up and coming round in hordes, singing Happy Birthday in an annoying way and showering her with presents but it did no good. In between visitors she stubbed her toe, discovered that she has grown too fat for her best dresses, felt sick and tired and would rather have been twenty-one. Or dead.

Her new blouse was a disappointment, her chocolate cake too dry and her new shoes too tight. Still the visitors trudged in and out with cards, flowers and presents, but they were mainly my friends, because most of my mother's friends are no more. So she battled with terminal depression until lunchtime. Then off we went to a charming café and ate salads in the sun and gradually my mother perked up. Only ten hours to go and the hated birthday would be over.

In fact in our house only the Daughter is wild about birthdays. She is eighteen and mad on partying. This year she hired a venue, invited hundreds and they all danced, drank heavily and screamed in a pit of hell until the early hours. I visited briefly and left with impaired hearing. What thrilled her particularly about this birthday was that she might officially drink herself under the table. To her a birthday means presents, luxury and being able officially to do what your mother has always told you not to do: leave school, earn money, fritter it, have sex, tattoo your whole body and marry a wastrel.

Now my birthday is looming, my waistline has left me for ever, the dog's time on earth is running out, but Rosemary is still nagging for some sort of celebration. She has recently embarked on a thrilling round of sixtieth birthday parties at which the food is exquisite because everyone is showing off how well they have done in life. Then together they all wander down memory lane while they still have some memory to speak of.

Secretly I am rather keen on birthdays. They show that I have somehow lasted fifty-four years. Only thirty-seven years to go and I too will have mobility and digestive problems. Rosemary is right. I should perhaps party while I still can.

NOT GOOD ENOUGH

Daughter has finished her A-levels. What a relief for all of us. This is a time that we have all longed for – a stress-free period when the Daughter and her peers, no longer burdened by homework and anxiety, will be free to help with washing-up, tidying, laundry, cooking and shopping. Tension and screaming in our home will stop and a generally sunny atmosphere will prevail.

For years I have clung to this dream like a drowning woman and at last it has come true. Daughter has been washing up, tidying and shopping *and* she has a job. But my mother is still not thrilled. She tends to clash with the Daughter over how much domestic work should be done by someone of eighteen. Their opinions differ wildly.

After years of slaving alone I am weedily grateful for any scrap of assistance in the home, but my mother is more demanding. Over the years she has noted the number of chores not done and it has rankled like a festering sore, reinfected after every meal and pile of laundry, until now, when the poison has surfaced like a giant boil, nearly bursting and not to be soothed by little patches of washing-up here and there.

The boil is further inflamed by my mother's own memories of childhood: her father a charming wastrel, gambling and disappearing, her mother slaving in a market, herself slogging away looking after the little brother and sister, her horrid home-made knitted red petticoats, the mockery at school. Now here is her grandchild swanning about town, her wardrobe immense, hair highlighted, mobile phone peeping and exotic holidays planned. To balance the books a huge amount of housework, drudgery and charming behaviour is required.

Foolishly I point out the improvement to my mother. 'Look,' I squeal, thrilled by the novelty. 'She's done the washing-up! She's hung up her clothes! Her room's tidy! She's got up and gone to work!'

'About time too,' roars my mother. 'I should bloody well think so.' She cannot get the hang of positive reinforcement. It is a new-fangled idea, miles across the generation crater and she cannot leap that far.

'Next time,' I instruct, 'Say *'How lovely. Thank you!'* Do not use a sarcastic tone.' My mother sneers rebelliously. Our home is still a war zone, the kitchen is the front line, with no chance of a stress-free life — just the occasional ceasefire. But I hope one day for a united household. Just another little dream of mine.

SAUSAGE ROLLS

My mother is off to a nursing home with a chum of hers. What bliss to get away from our home and its residents: my mess, the Daughter's UCAS stress, the dribbling dog and various annoying visitors. Instead she will have two weeks' tidiness, peace and her own peer group. It is called respite care.

Nowadays one has to be frightfully careful, what with all these hair-raising tales of the elderly being slapped about or scalded while their relatives aren't looking, but her friend Esther, after months of searching, has finally found somewhere suitable.

This is my mother's first proper break from the Household from Hell in over two years. She is thrilled. Off we go, out of town and into the fresh air. The chosen residence is surrounded by green lawns, the furnishings are tasteful, the rooms immaculate and staff charming. But wait! There is no bidet. My mother is bitterly disappointed. And a shower instead of a bath, and a slippery floor! Staff point out the special shower seat to soothe my mother, just in time for supper.

I accompany her to the dining room. The atmosphere is not vibrant. No one is chatting. Many are too poorly to chat. All residents are pallid. My mother is the only person with her lipstick on. Worse still, sausage rolls are on the menu. I suspect that sausage rolls might play havoc with an ancient digestive system, but they do tend to pop up on the menus of such establishments, together with white bread, moistureless chicken and wodgy puddings.

I leave my mother sitting bravely at the dining table and drive home in despair. Compare this British regime with the Pacific Home, California, where Rosemary's mother is spending half the year. Not a sausage roll in sight. Menu includes peach nectar, cinnamon toast, green beans on apple-walnut turkey, seafood basket, avocado salad and chicken wings and wine every Friday night. And an ocean front dining room, heated pool, sandy beach, billiards, library, Hobby Shop and other play areas. How depressing to find that the Pacific Home costs half the price of my mother's establishment. I am not pleased.

Next day I ring for a progress report.

'I told them where to stuff their sausage rolls,' roars my mother. Luckily bridge games have been organised and her chum has arrived. But will she last the fortnight? And will she ever speak to Rosemary's mother again?

SOS RESPITE

I ring my mother for a report on conditions in the nursing home in which I have so heartlessly left her. Grim news. The food continues fairly execrable and staff tell my mother that they are underpaid, overworked, and as from this week, may have no more free meals. Naturally they are mutinous and leaving in droves. No one has time to take my mother and her chum Esther downstairs and out into the sunny garden. For one week they have been marooned on the first floor.

As we chat on the telephone I hear wild and prolonged screaming in the background.

'Someone's screaming for help,' says my mother calmly. The screaming continues. No staff appear. We chatter on. Yesterday my mother ordered tomatoes vinaigrette, but the tomatoes appeared alone. More screaming. My mother is stuck in Colditz without a salad dressing. For this, we and the local council are paying £500 a week between us.

'Heee-eeellp,' goes the screaming. In desperation my mother prepares to investigate herself. Just in time a nurse appears. For £500 one can have one week full board in the charming Greek island hotel with turquoise swimming pool, where Daughter and I once spent a delightful holiday eating peaches and grapes for breakfast, and salads awash with dressing, day and night.

I may seem to be going overboard about salad dressings, but without a daily measure of olive oil, my mother's life is scarcely worth living. Also it is 1997, we are part of Europe and the days of yellow Salad Cream are meant to be over.

But my mother is determined to stick it out. She cannot desert her chum, who cannot go home because her daughter, who cares for her, is abroad on holiday. At least they have had two bridge games and some passable smoked mackerel. And they can chat non-stop.

Luckily Esther's other daughter has brought vital supplies of oil and taken them both out for tea. A sniff of open air at last. I hear that in HM Prisons, one hour daily in the open air is statutory. My mother might have been better off in Risley (cost=£480 per week, baths, bingo and all meals included). Perhaps she would like to escape early? Shall I collect her *before* the last lunch on Sunday?

'No!' my mother shouts defiantly. 'It's roast beef. I'm having it. I've bloody paid for it.' She has always been a determined woman.

THREE GENERATIONS

My friend Anne is in a tricky position. She is stuck between two rather confusing generations: the teenage son in her home and the very elderly mother up the road. Which one is a grown-up? She can never tell. Both need dinners and attention. The mother has nappies and tantrums, the son still needs food supplies and supervision. To his mind he is a grown-up but still needs assistance, especially with the mass catering, laundry and bed and breakfast facilities when his freinds come to visit.

What luck that her mother lives up the road. In our house my mother and daughter are crammed into the same premises. A teenager is a difficult creature to understand, especially from two generations away, so naturally things have been rather tense here, what with three generations of problems. Exams and romance, finance and household drudgery, arthritis and angina have all taken their toll and our home is now a tinderbox.

We desperately need a holiday each, but how? Easy enough for my daughter, free as a bird. She is off to Greece, but my mother's requirements are more complex: no stairs, charming company, full-time attendant, high-quality cuisine and fresh air.

Luckily she is able to escape on a mini holiday and so am I. She visits Ruislip, my childhood home, where my very old friend Jacqueline has her to stay. What a friend! She attends to my mother's every need for five days and provides visitors, delightful garden, home-grown produce and constant chat. My mother has a tremendous holiday. Five days without the rows, shrieking, vile language, tantrums, dribbling barking dog, streams of teenage visitors and layers of mess that makes life in our house a hell on earth. Meanwhile I am off for three days to the country with the dog. Bliss.

No wonder my mother looks tremendously well upon my return, her complexion glowing, her ankles slim, her mood light-hearted and optimistic. But once back in town her decline is rapid. The ankles swell, her strength and vitality go, and she retreats glumly to her bedroom. As night falls, troops of large and hulking visitors tramp past her door on the way to Granddaughter's room to do God knows what. My mother cannot rest. She knows that cigarettes are being smoked, the larder is emptying, the debris piling up and her grand-child hurtling down the road to ruin.

But all is not drear. Sometimes things lighten up in our house. One day Granddaughter behaves perfectly. She tidies, she washes up, she makes tea, she does homework, she bans visitors. But my mother cannot adapt to this sudden change. She cannot praise her grand-child. 'About bloody time too,' she snaps again, stamping into the garden.

Naturally my daughter is disappointed. 'Why is Grandma always horrid to me?' she cries and runs weeping to her room. My mother grumps about the garden, my daughter sobs upstairs. I find that on these occasions I tend to play football with the dog. Which is the grown-up in our house?

TRANSPORT

Transport for the elderly can be rather problematic. It is not easy getting my mother to the bank. Most banks are on high streets, protected from the immobile customer by double yellow lines and armies of traffic wardens. So for weeks I have postponed this outing, but my mother is dead keen to go.

At last we find ourselves on the High Street outside the chocolate shop. My mother is desperate for chocolate gingers. I am to dash in and buy them while she waits in the car. We are in a parking bay on a red route, but is it safe? On which side of the road may we park today and for how long?

'It's all right anywhere,' roars my mother with confidence. 'I've got my yellow badge.' She has forgotten that this is not Hove, but London, where life is brutal and harsh, criminals abound and law enforcement agencies are ruthless and sometimes even privatised. They know that my mother may be a vandal in disguise.

I rush to buy the chocs and return to find my mother chatting to a lady traffic warden in a friendly way about our bank problem. The warden assures her that we may park outside the bank freely with our disabled badge.

My mother is thrilled and now cannot be stopped. She must go to the bank. 'We can park there at any time,' says she defiantly. 'That nice lady warden said so.'

We go the very next day. Imagine our surprise as we stagger from the bank, to see a warden writing out a ticket. But this one isn't a charming lady. It is a white, pinched-face youth determined to book us. Blindly following the nice lady's instructions, we had failed to notice that one may not park here after four o'clock. It is now quarter past. Forty pounds fine.

My mother pleads and begs Pinchface to stop but he couldn't care. Were she to have a heart attack on the spot he would still issue his ticket, but my mother will try.

'Give up,' I yell coarsely from the car. 'You won't get anywhere. He couldn't give a *!*!*.' I am right, but it takes my mother some time to realise this. She repeats the instructions of the charming lady warden, she describes her infirmities, but to no avail, and our day is ruined.

Luckily we do not often need to visit high streets. My mother's lunch club is out of town and one can park in a carefree way. Bliss. Only this week I cannot take her. My car is in the garage. Never mind, we will book a taxi. My mother has a Taxi Card. We book it for 9.15 a.m.

Foolish innocents. The taxi fails to arrive. There is my mother, woken at dawn, struggled for two hours to get ready, waiting in her best clothes for her favourite weekly outing, and no taxi. I ring the taxi firm with these heart-rending details. They are unmoved.

'We haven't got one yet,' says the lady in charge, probably accustomed to moaning pensioners. 'We don't know when we'll have one. It does say on your card that this is not a guaranteed service.'

Transport facilities are obviously something of a lottery for the elderly. Our eighty-four-year-old chum is taken to and from her day centre by coach. The coach collects people alphabetically, which means driving all over London in large zig-zags, frequently passing within a whisker of our chum's street. She begs the driver to drop her there, but he won't. She must ziz-zag London for hours because her name begins with W.

Today I leave my mother waiting, chicly dressed, for her taxi, and stamp off for a dog walk. She is still there when I come back, resigned to her fate. I am in a foaming temper, but my mother is calm. She has become accustomed to transport cock-ups and waiting about like a bit of lost baggage. It is a part of growing old.

HOSPITAL

While I was out yesterday my mother had a horrid turn. Her eye began smarting and her left arm tingling, she called weakly for help but no one responded. Another drama was going on upstairs. Daughter had split her toe open, it poured blood, and while she screamed and searched wildly for plasters, her friends had carried on decorating upstairs, the pop music boomed on and no one could hear my mother. No wonder she panicked. The Grim Reaper could have snatched her away and no one would have been there to stop him.

Luckily I returned in the nick of time. The music was turned off, the toe stopped bleeding, the arm stopped tingling. A few hours of calm passed. Then the tingling started again. What a fright. I called the ambulance. Sometimes relaxation is not an option in our house. The tingling stopped. But the ambulance men were on their way. My mother tore off her rings again. She has taken to doing this whenever she feels suspiciously poorly. 'Take my rings,' she commanded with her remaining strength. 'Hide them.'

Two charming, calm and saintly ambulance men arrived, held my mother's hand, gave her breathing instructions and were ever so kind. Naturally she burst into tears. They would take her to hospital for a check-up. My mother perked up tremendously. Not only would she be safe, but she would also get out of our hell hole of a house for hours, maybe even days. She described our daily life in colourful detail to the ambulance men. They escorted her to the ambulance, all laughing and cracking jokes. I reminded my mother that she was meant to be ill, the National Health is run on a shoe-string and the neighbours might be watching and wondering. Could she please try to look a little more poorly?

She couldn't care. 'At least I'll be getting out of this ****house,' said she fiercely and staggered into the ambulance. Off she went to the Whittington. It was paradise. Everything was checked: chest X-rayed, blood pressure taken, heart monitored, pulses read, blood tested, consultants called. I followed later. My mother looked tremendously well. At 1.45 a.m. she was at last allowed home. She felt tip-top and waved happily at the receptionist on her way out.

'Another satisfied customer,' she called. The receptionist looked rather gobsmacked. Clients are rarely so cheery and appreciative. My mother will be back soon for a twenty-four-hour check-up. She cannot wait. In the meantime she has had a thrilling evening, the Reaper has buzzed off, the weather is improving and the rings have gone on again. We live on a roller coaster.

TERRIBLE FUTURE

A terrible sense of emptiness hit me the other day. There is not a single costume drama left on telly. Over the last year I have come to rely on them – the period frocks, the bonnets, horses, carriages and country houses, charming manners, witty chat, repressed sex and happy endings. I need at least one hour of it on Sundays to get me through the week.

Perhaps I am wallowing in the past because the present and future look rather bleak. Rosemary and I realised the other day that we are lucky to be over fifty and shall be dead before things get much worse.

As we walked the dog round the block the other night we noticed that many windows on the top floors of the houses were open, despite the bitter weather, and teenagers were hanging out of them puffing various sorts of smoke into the freezing night air and wasting the central heating. Rosemary and I suspected marijuana.

Apparently the children are under great stress nowadays and no wonder. The world is going down the drain and they must go with it. Here we are plagued by Third World debt, pollution, corruption, festering mountains of nuclear waste, rampaging new diseases, poisoned hamburgers and Andrew Lloyd Webber musicals. No wonder today's youth seem rather wild.

And our house is alive with teenagers. This is hell for my mother, especially at weekends when the Daughter's chums stream through the house, clomping up and down the stairs past her bedroom. She sees the long or matted hair, the skateboards, the raggedy clothes, hears the noise, foul language and thumping music and smells the ciggy smoke, and naturally it sets her shouting.

'Who the bloody hell is that?' she roars. 'No smoking in this house.' The youths tiptoe up and down, my mother shoots out of her room like the troll under the Billy Goats' bridge, defending our home. To her they are not some other mothers' babies in a stressful world, but big strange men, many of whom clump downstairs again and use her lavatory. If there's anything my mother cannot bear, it is a strange man's bottom on her lavatory. And she has taken to hiding the candelabra. What if a youth should spot it gleaming in her bedroom and make off with it? She lives on a knife edge.

Who can blame her? The young are a strange lot. Things were much pleasanter in our day. We went to bed earlier, did more homework, knew our tables, had better pop songs, better clothes and less dangerous habits. Soon we will be the stuff of costume dramas.

GALLEY SLAVES

My mother is still the resident chef. Thank goodness. I am increasingly sick to death of cooking and the kitchen. Today she staggered downstairs to make chicken soup, one of her specialities.

'What will you do when I'm dead?' she cried, leaning exhausted on the draining board. 'What will you eat?'

'Vegetarian snacks, uncooked.'

'What about *her*,' groans my mother, referring to her voracious granddaughter. 'She'll want dinners.'

But by the time my mother is departed, the granddaughter will have left college and have time to slave over her own meals. I shall insist that she does so. This is my new resolution.

My mother has no confidence in it. She feels that my authority over the Daughter is negligible, so she battles on with the cooking, knowing that should she stop we will all revert to eating rubbish snacks, become anaemic and succumb to disease. This is her fate – to drag herself about until the very end, ensuring that her two infants are adequately fed.

To the outsider I may seem heartless and wicked, forcing my ninety-year-old mother to be galley slave, but surprisingly, she is still keen on cooking. I cannot understand why. Even Rosemary has begun to find it tiresome. For years she has cooked vigorously, and even, when her husband was alive, regularly produced three contrasting meals at once: curry for the husband, non-curry for the son and vegetarian delicacies for the daughters. She herself would pick at bits of everyone else's dinner. But now she can scarcely be bothered.

On Sunday I took my mother to visit my old friend Jacqueline for lunch. She too has spent thirty-five years sweating in the kitchen, catering for her husband and three children. What bad luck that my mother has brought fish-cake ingredients with her. After lunch she springs up and begins cooking away with Jacqueline as assistant. Soon they both stagger from the kitchen, eyes watering from the grated onions and both stinking of fried fish. It rather got up my mother's nose that I was relaxing in front of *EastEnders* omnibus, but I have had the fish-cake lesson and experience countless times and it is my day off.

This has been a disappointing area of my mother's life, to have had a sullen daughter who scuttles away when recipes are mentioned. But what if I had loved cooking and we had been in competition? One thing I do appreciate about a kitchen – you can only have one head chef.

THE OLD COUNTRY – HOVE

My mother and I are off to Hove to visit all the old friends she now never sees and the crematorium and Garden of Remembrance where my father lies sprinkled round a rose bush.

I have not been looking forward to this trip. The drive is long and exhausting, hordes of friends must be fitted in and I am apt to blub at even the thought of the crematorium and bawl at the sight of a written memorial, even to an unknown cat, never mind my own father. I avoid reading the little plaque under the rose bush and fiddle about moving the car into the shade, otherwise the dog will expire from the heat and make our day out even more tragic.

My mother is keen to sit in the rose garden for hours, dead-heading the roses and chatting to the assistant but we must speed on with our visiting schedule. My mother's friends are thrilled to see her at last and have cancelled their bridge games en masse without a second thought. No other action could so clearly convince my mother of her own worth and their devotion.

The sun blazes down, we sit on sunny patios and flowered balconies, eat a divine lunch, drink tea and hear of all the scandals, bits of bad behaviour and deaths that have occurred since my mother left this seaside heaven and came to live in stinking London.

Her friend Betty shows my mother the next-door flat. It is empty. It has French windows opening on to Betty's divine garden and was designed in heaven for my mother. And only £50 a week!

My mother gazes at it wistfully. It is utterly perfect but two years too late. If only it had been there when she first thought of moving, then she would have been in it like a shot, but now she has grown accustomed to our London hell hole. It has its advantages: me, the nearby hospital, the saintly social worker and her dream-boat doctor.

She dare not leave them. Bitter memories of the south coast still plague her: the overworked doctors, insolent receptionists and my father's last grim and neglected days in the local hospital, our own personal Death Row. No amount of bridge games, chums and sunny patios can dispel the terror of this final threat. Our house is now her home – for better or worse.

ACCIDENTS

I am still hobbling around in a sock, scarcely recovered from a horrible sprained ankle, when Rosemary falls down the stairs and breaks hers. We are going down like ninepins over here, the house littered with crutches and our elderly limbs snapping like twigs. There is Rosemary sitting on the stairs holding up her oddly shaped purple ankle. She cannot even bear to dangle it.

Off we all go to hospital. It is like a war zone, flooded with spilt coffee, injured persons sprawling about and a pale lady, possibly homeless, with tatty hair and mottled legs, stuck blankly in a wheechair. Emergencies have been flooding in and waiting time is six hours.

Still Rosemary is polite and stoical. 'Poor girl,' says she, looking at the exhausted and overworked nurse. 'This is no longer a rewarding job.' Rosemary's daughter and I leave her here in hell where she waits until 4 a.m. to have her leg plastered, unsuccessfully and without a painkiller. There are not enough staff to supervise it. Next day she must have an operation.

But has she told them of her sleep apnoea? No. I order her to do so. One can take stoicism too far. Suppose her throat closes up mid-op? I am desperate not to have another funeral in our street. Death is creeping nearer and starting to nibble at my friends and acquaintances, and during Rosemary's overnight wait, the flesh-eating virus gobbled someone up in the hospital.

I visit Rosemary after her operation. Her leg looks a fright, and the other one, the 'jealous leg', is covered in a chic white elastic stocking, *and* she has a non-slip bootee and exercise strip. I am rather envious. Trust her to go one better than me and be cosseted, but she was polite to hospital staff, whereas I had a tantrum after a mere four-hour wait. We have a desperate and bitter laugh about it. Rosemary grows more serene with age, while I grow more obnoxious. But here is a chance for me to be pleasant. I can now do Rosemary's shopping and chauffeuring for three months, helped by her three saintly children.

This drama has terrified my mother. 'This is Cripplegate,' she cries and glues herself to the phone warning her friends not to hurry downstairs with the ironing board, as Rosemary did. She watches my movements like a hawk. 'Make sure you have a hand free!' she screams. 'Hold on to the bannisters!' Who says the elderly have dull lives?

BOLD PROGRAMMES

I return from my morning dog walk to find my mother glued to the television. 'They're talking about sex again,' says she, thrilled to bits. 'Yesterday it was women, today it's men. The men are better.' An Italian and an Englishman are squabbling over indigenous approaches to love. And all this straight after breakfast.

My mother is stunned by this sudden rash of bold television programmes. Only last week we turned on the telly to watch some innocuous programme and inadvertently caught the end of another one about men. There was a penis, growing larger by the second.

'Bloody hell,' roared my mother, shocked to the core. 'Disgusting!' She cannot get over how rude the telly has become. There was a time when one never saw anyone's bottom, male or female, back or front, upon the screen. She has had to adapt tremendously, but is learning to go with the flow.

'It's orgasms *again*,' she shouts this morning from her bedroom. Concern about men's health is rife and orgasms are all the rage at present and have been for some time. People are demanding them left, right and centre, with sensitivity, of course. No wonder men are flagging. In my mother's youth people did not talk openly about such topics.

Perhaps they should have done. It is always sensible to compare and contrast, otherwise how do you find out what you're missing? Not that I want to generalise, and millions of people probably find orgasms a walkover from the word go, but some women discover them late in life. After years of dull relationships, they find a new partner, man or woman, who rather perks things up.

This seems to happen from the late thirties onwards. 'I used to wonder what all the fuss was about,' says my friend X. For years she plodded on with this rather dreary performance with the husband, wondering what everyone else was talking about. Could it be the same activity? Then suddenly along came a new chap and the world lit up. She could scarcely move a step without an orgasm. Lucky she. Here is a pastime that can obviously improve with age.

This may in part be due to the efforts of men. They are sometimes, when older, apt to make rather more effort, if one demands it of them. My friend Fielding is forever wondering what to do for the best. People come and go with contrasting theories, rather like the Schools Inspectorate, and, unable to rely any longer on the vigour and charms of youth, he battles to keep up with them. A youth would never bother. Even if he wanted to, he might not dare. This area is something of a minefield for the beginner.

Perhaps Fielding should be thrilled that he is now elderly and may, if he chooses, give up on the whole thing. No one will laugh. In later life this move is often applauded rather than sneered at. But youth has no such choice. They are under great pressure to be wild. I remember being cruelly mocked at Art School in the sixties for being rather late off the mark. There was everyone wallowing in sex and drugs, and there was I practising the piano. This was a grim time for me.

Meanwhile my mother keeps me up to date with the televised details. 'This man's twenty-three, he's never done it and he wants to wait till he's married and they're all laughing at him.' My mother laughs with them in a somewhat contemptuous and ribald way. She at least grows more and more enlightened with age.

THREE MOTHERS

Rosemary tells me that three of her friends have come up with a gem of an idea for their elderly mothers. They have bought a rambling property out in Norfolk and are about to install the mothers in it. Social services are thrilled. Three of their clients, formerly scattered all over the county can now all be visited in one swoop.

For now the daughters will all visit the mothers in shifts, but they have cleverly applied for early retirement. Then they will all move into the rambling property, the ancient mothers will eventually fade out and the three friends take their places, grow old and live happily together to the end. But first of all they are going to train the mothers to play bridge, eat pleasantly together at table and like each other.

Ha ha. Some hopes. Rosemary and I have tried to make our mothers be friends but they will not oblige. It is bad enough forcing your child to play with your friends' children, never mind making your mothers chum up. Olga and I tried to combine our children when they were teeny. They whacked each other with robots, fought over the Wendy house and grew up to regard each other with disdain.

Meanwhile my mother is the most rebellious. She was horrified to find that Rosemary's mother is frittering her money on herself, rather than handing it over to her struggling widowed daughter. Here is my mother scrimping and saving it all for me, and there is Rosemary's mother relaxing on holiday in San Francisco while Rosemary slaves away in the inner city. She now finds fault with Rosemary's mother's every word, action, movement or breath.

'What do I want a letter from *her* for,' shouts my mother in a fury. 'Why do I want to know what *she's* doing?' Rosemary's mother kindly sends cards and regards to my mother, and this is the response she gets. We keep my mother's behaviour a secret. Imagine the two of them banged up together in Norfolk.

Perhaps the other three mothers could be placed in perimeter cottages while the daughters share the central mansion. Or perhaps our own mothers are just not a good match. Mine is bold, forthright and rarely quiet; Rosemary's is a polite Christian. Other mothers may be better behaved.

Meanwhile Rosemary's mother rather envies mine. If my mother can live with me, why can't she live with Rosemary? My mother has described the hell on earth that is living with one's daughter, but Rosemary's cannot believe it. This envy could easily turn to loathing. We will not be searching for a large property in the country.

CRUTCHES

Weeks have passed and still Rosemary has not got the hang of her crutches and avoids physiotherapy. 'Come and look,' she shouts, 'one leg is withered and the other's like a tree trunk!' She has taken to gazing at her withered limb and stroking it lovingly. She is a fearfully annoying patient.

Off we went again to the charming nurses at our health centre so they could attend to the suppurating leg and hopefully give Rosemary a telling-off. We had a little squabble in the waiting room as Rosemary doddered about on her crutches and I heartlessly ordered her to hurry up.

'Shut up and get me a ticket,' roared Rosemary, lashing out with a crutch. The other waiting patients were thrilled by our spat. There is nothing better, when one is stuck for hours in a doctor's waiting room, than to be diverted by other patients behaving badly, especially if they are mature grown-ups and meant to know better.

'What about a hot chocolate?' I asked Rosemary, trying to be pleasant, but the drinks machine was broken.

'You said that on purpose,' she snapped, 'just so I'd be disappointed.'

Just in time the nurse arrived. 'Give her a crutch lesson,' I shouted. 'She will *not* do as she's told!'

'She's doing very nicely,' said the nurse and led Rosemary away to be pampered. But Rosemary and I made up on the way home. We always do. My mother is sick to death of it.

'You're always at *her* house,' she roars. 'Why don't you two get married?' Yesterday she suspected that I had been visiting Rosemary even before making the breakfast. There was my mother, lying in bed starving, and me off negligently playing with my friend next door, but she was wrong. I had been innocently walking the dog.

Naturally Rosemary tried to appease my mother by giving her the Zimmer frame, a real sacrifice considering her difficulty with the crutches, but my mother rejected it out of hand.

'It's no bloody good to me,' she shouted. 'It hasn't got wheels.'

Then Rosemary swapped her car for an automatic and drove my mother all the way to her bridge game, so that I could relax at home. It made her leg throb terribly, and me feel guilty, but it was worth it. It silenced my mother for days, so that Rosemary and I could squabble freely.

TURKEY HALVES

Rosemary and I never did get to spend Christmas together. We had one divine morning on the sunny Heath with the dog planning it, then things went suddenly and horribly wrong. First Rosemary lost her car keys somewhere in the grass and we couldn't get home. Daughter had to be called to fetch us and my family turned against Rosemary, for losing keys and borrowing our table.

Actually, Rosemary had done nothing wrong, but this was the pre-Christmas period when people are brewing up for festive tempers and she just happened to be in the way. So she chickened out of the shared Christmas. And she wasn't the only one to panic. Concerned neighbours, hearing of our plan, invited Rosemary's son to Christmas lunch with them, to save him from hell.

But by now Rosemary and I had already ordered our turkey. What were we to do? There was only one solution. Cut the turkey in half. I ran round to tell the butcher. He had known of the risks but was hoping for the best.

'Yes or no?' asked Butcher anxiously.

No. Butcher had to chop the turkey into two. 'It'll be fine,' said he looking worried, and wrapped the halves up neatly. 'Just keep basting it,' he cried rather poignantly. 'Happy Christmas!'

If only. The Daughter adores Christmas and had been busy for weeks, decorating, arranging twinkly lights and pretty cards, sprinkling cranberries about, shopping, shopping and shopping. But my mother loathes the whole performance. She is still waiting for the Messiah to come.

'Happy Christmas!' cried the Daughter cheerily on Christmas morning.

'I wish I'd died in the night,' groaned my mother, setting the tone for the day, then she staggered to the kitchen to make chestnut stuffing, Daughter and I battled on with the cooking, extra basting, presents, lighting fires, being cheery, but there was no escaping our tradition of an Xmas-day scream. It happened just before lunch, for no specific reason. It's just that all the year's aggravation had been simmering away and this is when it tends to erupt like Montserrat and foul up the festivities. Rosemary had a lucky escape. But we pressed on, our half turkey was heavenly, we all wore our new presents, visited neighbours for tea, things calmed down, Rosemary and I are still friends and the dog wasn't even sick. A triumph by our standards.

DESPAIR

The cold is turning my mother into a slug-a-bed. She has not left the house for days and lies endlessly watching telly. Last week I found her gripped by a programme on euthanasia.

'Would you do that for me?' she asked glumly.

I told her I might have to go to prison for murder but she was unmoved. She is not the only one. My friend Sylvia is also fed up with the weather. She hasn't looked upwards for weeks. Why bother? She is sick of looking at the endless grey. We had a short euthanasia debate on our dog walk. Sylvia too has been contemplating death and has written a Living Will. And if the doctors here refuse to do as they're told, then she'll be off to Holland.

'I have lots of friends there,' says she, 'and it's much nearer than Australia.'

'Will the friends be lined up with their cushions?'

Sylvia won't say, but she is determined. My mother is cheered to think that she is not the only one contemplating suicide. She changes her mind and makes some fish-cakes instead.

Just in case she sinks into another gloom, I force her to get up next day and attend her bridge club. Bridge is a dangerous game that she plays every Wednesday. The room is hot, the noise deafening and every table packed with players prey to outbursts of temper, bad behaviour and rudeness that would never be tolerated elsewhere. The room simmers with repressed loathing. Often the loathing bursts out.

'I'm not playing with that horrible man,' shouted my mother last week. 'I come here to RELAX.' By teatime her nerves were in shreds. I arrived to find her on the brink of a fight. She had been guarding her friend's seat in the tea room when along came another old lady and sat in it without so much as a by your leave.

'Do you mind!' roared my mother. 'This is my friend's chair and I'm saving it.'

'Well, it's my chair now,' said the rude lady, and just in the nick of time, back came the friend and elbowed/Zimmer-framed the interloper out of the way.

'Bloody old COW,' said my mother, in what she thought was an undertone, but the lady whipped round in a fury.

'What did you say?' she snapped fiercely. The tea room fell silent. Would there be bloodshed?

'I said "I don't want a ROW",' lied my mother, cleverly emphasising the rhyming word. Off lumbered the deposed woman and along came the tea and cake trolley. My mother couldn't wait to get back to bed and the telly. It is, she now realises, a delightful option.

OTHER FAMILIES

My mother returns from her club in a joyous mood. This woman she's never spoken to before suddenly started chatting and bemoaning her daughter's and granddaughter's behaviour. Both address her disrespectfully and use vile language.

'Your daughter?' asked my mother, horrified. 'Granddaughter yes, but daughter, *No*! My daughter would *never* speak to me like that!'

This was a treat for my mother. Usually it is other women gaping at her saying, 'My granddaughter would *never* behave like that!', or staring as if shell-shocked at my clothing or coiffure. But I have now become a paragon in her eyes. It is sometimes uplifting to hear that others are worse off than yourself.

My friend Jacqueline's mother suddenly fell down while pottering round the garden and broke her arm. She has now come to stay with Jacqueline to be looked after. But what bad luck: just as she moved in the builders moved out, halfway through the job, as builders are wont to do, and left them without a kitchen.

Jacqueline now has no oven and her family and temporarily disabled mother live on a building site. Still, she is doing her best, and this weekend barbecued the dinner, peeled her mother's new potatoes, as requested, cut up the meat lovely and small and carried it up on a tray.

'Where's the gravy?' asked her mother crossly. She will only accept conventional dinners and anything wildly out of the ordinary, like rice, is rejected out of hand.

My mother is thrilled by all this. Compared to Jacqueline's mother she is tremendously easy-going and will eat all manner of adventurous dinners without complaint. She now shouts 'Where's the gravy?' in a mocking way at the beginning of every meal and will brook no criticism of her own family.

Yesterday Rosemary unwisely criticised my celery and walnut soup. She had contributed a celery and come to collect her portion, just as my mother was drinking hers. 'Tastes of nothing,' said my mother disdainfully. 'Where's the soy sauce?'

Rosemary tasted it. A stark choice loomed. She must agree with me or my mother. Unwisely she chose to suck up to my mother and agreed with her criticism. Wrong. My mother managed to contain herself until Rosemary had gone home, then she let rip.

'She can make her own bloody soup if she doesn't like it!' she yelled, drinking up the ghastly stuff. 'Where's the salt?' she moaned, screwing up her nose. 'Don't make this again. It's very bland.' She glared defiantly. 'No one can criticise my daughter,' she snapped, 'except me.'

THE FEUD

This is a delicate subject, but Rosemary and my mother haven't spoken to each other since before Christmas when they fell out over Rosemary's lost keys, the half turkey and our table that Rosemary had borrowed. There have been moments over the last few months when they could have made up – when they passed in the hall or on the pavement, but then my mother, taken by surprise, would do a quick, semi-automatic glare and Rosemary would ice over and the moment would pass.

As time went by, the glare fixed and the ice thickened, positions became entrenched and hope of an end to hostilities seemed to fade. Because the trouble is, we have two champions here. My mother has had ninety-two years of grudge practice, but in sixty years Rosemary has also built up a very impressive portfolio. Numerous people have committed major or minor misdemeanours and Rosemary has never quite been able to forgive them. Sometimes she can't quite remember what for. There's the butcher, a couple of ex-colleagues, a vicar, a friend in Yorkshire. Rosemary has avoided the whole of Yorkshire for years, because once she turns, she turns for good.

'You never realised I could do it too!' says she defiantly. But then at last, along comes a common enemy – the hairdresser. Today she is three and a half hours late. My mother and Rosemary meet in the hall and have a shout together about it. United at last, we hope. Poor Hairdresser is always late – because of the traffic, migraine, the car breaking down, her mother, her son, the builders. Her life is hell. Our house makes it worse.

Usually I remain neutral, and when things become really tense indoors, I go and stare at the frogs in our pond. This is a fantastic time of year for my frogs who have been thrashing around out there croaking and squeezing each other since February, especially on warm sunny days. But sometimes a horrible silence hangs over the pond, and this morning Gardener found two sad little frog corpses on the lawn. The cats have been marauding, *and one of them is Rosemary's.*

'He toys with them,' says she airily, 'tossing them into the air and then dragging them into the living room.' Oh, really? And what was that about some keys, a half turkey and a table?

GARDENING TO THE END

As I grow older and older I become more and more keen on the garden. It is a scented paradised enhanced by bird song and the croaking of froggies from the pond. A charming exodus of witsy, baby frogs jumps diagonally across the lawn and bees hum about the flowers. To reach this heaven I need only shuffle a few steps from my kitchen door.

No wonder the elderly are prone to gardening. Last year's Chelsea show was chock-full of them, Rosemary and Olga and Sylvia are endlessly fiddling in their gardens and so is my mother.

But a garden can be a dangerous emotional minefield. My mother and I are forever battling over choice of plants and methods. I move her favourite poppies, she hacks at my favourite rose bush. There it is hanging gracefully over the pond, I go shopping briefly, I return to find it looking like a mad person's haircut. Rosemary gangs up with my mother. 'Nothing wrong with it,' she snaps. 'I don't know what you're on about.' She perhaps envies my alstroemeria. It is more attractively coloured than hers.

And now the runner beans are climbing over the wall. My mother now fears that the neighbour, who we don't like, may get some of our beans. This cannot happen. The beans must be redirected. And the other neighbour, who we do like, has allowed his convolvulus to rampage all over our roses. Soon my mother's patience will snap and she will never lend him the bottle-opener again.

Things are even worse for Rosemary. She has been forced to build a large trellis on one side to block off the neighbour who will keep on chatting and relentlessly singing along to hymns. But Rosemary's water lily has flowered and mine hasn't, although we bought them at the same time in the same place. I am furious.

Our gardens are fraught with tension and under constant threat. Squirrels have chewed the tops off Rosemary's pinks, eaten my strawberries and torn up my thyme, cats have pooed on my newly planted rudbeckia, the dog has weed on the lawn and the snails are champing through everything.

In fact the garden is a battle ground. Over it one can fight one's friends, relatives, neighbours, Gardener and the elements. It develops diseases, attracts pests, causes rows, needs constant attention and is all-consuming. We need never go anywhere else.

CRUMBLING AWAY

Last week my mother had an appointment at the rheumatology clinic because her legs don't work properly any more. She was desperate to go, even with her ghastly backache. What a vile time we had, stuck in hospital for ever while outside the sun blazed down and the only day of summer passed by. Inside we waited. And waited and waited, my mother occasionally screaming with pain, me stamping about in a temper.

After two and a half hours of nothing I phoned Rosemary weeping with fury. She dashed to the hospital at once for a coffee break and took charge. 'Stop this at once!' said she, out in the sun with our coffees. 'It's like having an infant beside me. Once you're here, you have to go into a time warp. That's what I do. You're behaviour is appalling.' My mother's behaviour was much better than mine. She just waited in the X-ray department, moaning and growing paler.

But what a good job we went. Her back wasn't strained, it had crumbled. She has osteoporosis and three vertebrae have gone for a burton. No wonder she's been screaming for weeks. And there was I thinking it was only a pulled muscle, bossing my mother about and thinking her a fuss-pot. Now I feel like a Nazi.

'This won't last for ever,' said the doctor, and mentioned that it was a pity she hadn't been given HRT years ago. But years ago my mother lived on the south coast, where the elderly live in their squillions, and when a county is clogged to bursting with crumbling pensioners, it tends not to look to the future, possibly hoping that they haven't a future worth bothering about. Why waste money on HRT? So here is my mother, ninety-two, bones crumbling and more of a mess to sort out.

And when she'd had her X-ray, her blood tests, the X-ray result and verdict, we could go home at last. Nurses will come daily and give her injections. My mother reached her bedroom ashen after five hours in the hospital, still crippled but in a more relaxed mood. At last everybody appreciates her reason for screaming.

'I don't scream for nothing,' says she grimly. Absolutely. Now where is my nice pot of natural yam progesterone cream? Will it work? I expect I'll find out when I'm ninety-two.

CATARACT QUEUE

My mother is on the cataract waiting list. As it's meant to be six months long and she's been waiting seven, perhaps she'll be nearing the top. I ring to find out.

'Your mother is not an urgent case,' says the list organiser. 'She's routine.' Well, of course. My mother's ninety-two, completely blind in one eye, can only read huge print, must sit two inches from the telly, keeps bumping into things and can't find her false teeth. She is to spend the remainder of her time on earth tottering about in a mist.

But we are in luck. As she has osteoporosis and has just recovered from a crumbling broken back, it is imperative that she doesn't bump into things and fall over. The back specialist writes to the eye specialist to see if she can be made a priority. He dictates this letter as we watch. Bliss. Things are on the move.

Eight days pass. I ring the eye department. They have heard nothing from the back specialist. My mother is still mouldering at the bottom of the list. Why? Oh, it takes two weeks for a letter to arrive, be seen, shown to the specialist and a decision to be made. But the letter hasn't even arrived yet. And anyway, the waiting list isn't six months, it's a year.

With any luck, if you put a ninety-two-year-old woman on a year-long waiting list, she'll drop dead before she gets to the top, saving the NHS time and money. Meanwhile, where is the back specialist's letter?

No one has seen it. My mother's file is not in the normal place. A search is carried out, the file found, the letter discovered. It will be typed out at once and faxed to the eye consultant. Poor Secretary has three consultants' work to do and hasn't had time to do it yet. Now we're short of midwives, nurses *and* medical secretaries. Next day I track the fax down. It has gone to another secretary who kindly whacks it into the eye consultant's tray with our request underlined in red.

But consultant is away until next week. Then she may decide whether my mother, one among hundreds of fading, semi-blind elderly patients, should become a priority. And we live in the First World.

This operation costs £2–3000 privately. Apparently Marxism is making a comeback. Not a moment too soon.

EYEBALLS

It is all eyeballs in our house. The dog's eyeball has festered for months and now my mother has finally had her cataract operation. With a local anaesthetic. Ow. She saw it coming. And her ward was plastered with technicolour eyeball pictures.

It has been a difficult time for me because I'm not keen on eyeballs. The thought of anything happening to an eyeball makes me break out into a boiling sweat, except for my legs, which go icy cold and shrink. In this condition I must put my mother's eye drops in four times a day. To help things along I have a shout just before the drops. Aaaargh! Naturally my mother is hurt.

'You don't mind the dog's eyeball,' says she poignantly. 'What's so terrible about mine?' But the dog's eyeball is plain brown and looks rather more robust. My mother's looks delicate and more like a bare eyeball.

And it isn't only eyeballs. As the years pass by I am growing more and more vapourish. Any glimpse of physical injury will do it – any blood on telly, any suggestion of knives or razors and I'm sweating and fainting again. Any births, deaths, wars, catastrophes or unfortunate animals and I'm blubbing away. To avoid mockery, I watch *Pet Rescue* alone in my bedroom where I can cry undisturbed.

'It's your menopause,' says Rosemary strictly. 'It's a transitional phase. You'll be better soon.' But she's wrong. Phases don't last for twenty-five years. I ring my friend Fielding for a change of topic, but bad luck. He has just been to the eye hospital to have two styes-turned-cysts removed.

'It was Duke of Gloucester Ward!' he shouts, and describes the operation, which he remembered in detail, thanks to local anaesthetic. His eyelids were stuck with daggers and knives, then he was sent home, bandaged and bleeding, in a taxi. Taxi driver had to lead him to his garden gate and open his front door for him and his daughter won't come home because he looks such a fright. She is staying elsewhere. Feeling rather hurt, Fielding sank on to the sofa and turned the telly on for some football, but his eyes were veiled in blood and bandages and he couldn't watch it, which has wrecked his holidays. But at least my mother can now thread a needle without her glasses on. Happy New Year.

BOTTOM WIPER

We arrive at the Heath in the car. The dog and I leap out and leave Rosemary to lock her side, but I hear that the door hasn't shut correctly. 'Is it locked properly?' I ask. Rosemary is incensed. 'How dare you?' she roars. 'I have locked this door hundreds of times, I am perfectly capable of doing it, and you are a *bottom wiper!*'

What will the public out for their Saturday walks think? Will they realise that this is a metaphor? 'You are always doing this!' Rosemary rants on. 'You don't trust anyone to do anything properly, you're always checking up!'

She doesn't understand that it's anxiety, not mistrust. How can I be sure that she'll turn my oven off when I'm out, call in on my mother, save my Sunday paper, draw my blinds when I'm away? In her place I would forget. I did yesterday.

I was meant to defrost Rosemary's casserole in my microwave, but I forgot. Twenty minutes later, her guests eagerly awaiting their dinner, Rosemary rang. She should have rung much earlier to check. I wouldn't have minded, because I'm used to anxious and fastidious bottom wipers. My mother is one.

Rosemary's mummy probably let her get on with things, but my mummy worried and supervised over clean bottoms for longer than average. She still does, metaphorically of course. 'Have you turned the oven off?' she calls. 'Have you locked the door/put the chicken in the fridge/turned the bath off/phoned the bank/put salt on the fish/found the bridge table?'

'Yes, yes, yes, yes, yes, yes, yes.'

'Are you sure?/Have you checked?/How much?/When?/Show me.'

'Yes, yes, yes, yes, all right.'

And then, perhaps overwhelmed and confused by the spray of

bullet questions, I may forget something, so my mother's anxiety is reinforced and she checks and questions all the more. So imagine my surprise at Rosemary's outburst over my one weedy little question. It reminded her of all my other little questions over the years and she is still furious.

This is the wonderful thing about a dog, especially for a metaphorical bottom wiper. I can't say it often enough. You can supervise it and check and look after its physical needs for ever and ever amen until it is quite grown up and nobody minds. And, if absolutely necessary, you can even wipe its bottom.

INSOMNIA

My mother is glued to *Teletubbies* again this morning. 'Tinky Winky can't sleep,' she cries sympathetically. He is not the only one. In our house we have been waking up at 3 a.m. and lying about in a temper till dawn. Then we fall asleep just in time to get up again and start the day with our eyes starting out of our head and brains scrambled, totter around feeling slightly demented until 3 p.m. and then start falling asleep again.

This is a common problem at our age, says Fielding. He keeps headphones at his bedside so he can clamp them on and listen to the World Service or Five Live for hours on end until he falls asleep. Then he staggers to work, where he spots all the other insomniacs by their heads drooping and jerking in staff meetings.

Apparently, the thing to do is not to get cross or worry. It's the rage that's exhausting, not the lack of sleep, so I am told. But in the early hours, everything is worrying. In the silence I can hear my brain crackling away dredging up regrets and forecasting doom.

So I have given up tea or coffee after 1 p.m., drink only camomile or peppermint infusions. I sprinkle lavender on the pillow, read dull books, have relaxing baths, and try not to worry. Nothing works.

After my little stay in hospital, I had begun to sleep like a log, but yesterday morning I was woken at five-thirty by the dog, desperate to go out and be sick in the garden. Which woke my mother up on one of the few mornings when she was fast asleep.

Then this morning the dog started bumbling about again. Did it have insomnia? It was staggering around like a drunk, sniffing randomly, banging into things, jerking and trembling. Brain tumour, I thought straightaway. It tottered downstairs on its rubber legs with me holding its wobbly body upright. Was this the end? Please not.

No, it was a fit. The dog has low blood sugar. It is on steroids. Steroids make her pee on the bed, the sofa, the armchairs and the carpets. The whole house is swathed in plastic, everything rustles. Will we ever sleep again?

RECOVERY

My mother has recovered from her hideous crumbly-back illness. What a relief. When someone is ninety-two and ever so poorly, it is difficult to imagine that they will ever recover. So while my mother and I have plodded through this ghastly ordeal, we have each been secretly planning funerals and expecting the Reaper to call any minute.

I have gone off for my dog walkies in the morning leaving my mother asleep. There she was, looking white, deathly and motionless. Was she still with us? Should I wake her and find out? Will she still be here after my walkie? Meanwhile my mother was expecting to leave this earth at about four in the morning. Forty-four was my father's favourite number, and as she often finds herself awake at about that time, she's been hoping he might call for her at about 4.44 a.m. and escort her to wherever it is that one goes.

'You never go alone,' says she mysteriously. Luckily my mother wasn't going anywhere, except out of bed and down into the sunny garden. After four weeks of hell she has started tottering around again and is even contemplating some more bridge and cooking. But we still live on a knife edge. This broiling weather is dangerous for the elderly. I heard it on telly. The winter was perilous, now the summer is perilous. My mother must keep out of the sun and drink gallons.

We shunt her around the cooler parts of the house until the evening, when she staggers out for a mini-walk along the pavement. But although things are looking up, she is worrying about her rings again. The first thing I must be sure to do before she is whisked away in the ambulance is to take them off, just in case a passing robber whips them from her hand as it dangles helplessly from some god-forsaken hospital trolley.

But what will I do with them once I've saved them? 'You said you didn't like them,' cries my mother in a heart-rending way. But I do. I don't remember saying that. I love the rings. Then what if I lose them? Another huge area of anxiety is looming. Hopefully it can be postponed for some time. Each morning I look into her bedroom. Is she breathing? Yes.

'I'm still here!' croaks my mother, every time.

ZIMMER

My mother has set her heart on a three-wheel Zimmer frame on which she can scoot along the pavement, rather than the sort she has to pick up and plonk down all the time. The very lovely three-wheel folding ones are available in a big chemist in central London.

We ring to make sure they have one. 'Yes. We always have one for you to try,' says the chemist woman, so off we go, on a Saturday afternoon in the searing heat and get stuck in a 'Reclaim the Streets' traffic jam. Or is it a bomb in Camden? Reports vary. My mother is quaking in her seat. And this was meant to be a pleasant outing. She imagined herself perhaps having delightful tea and cakes at Sagné's in Marylebone Road, a divine patisserie that she remembers from her youth. Instead we are sweltering in traffic.

At last we reach the chemist's. You guessed it. No Zimmer.

'What is Zimmer?' asks a baffled assistant. Another assistant goes to search for one. 'Zimmer's gone out of business,' says she. Meanwhile, I buy my mother a footbath for her birthday on Wednesday. 'Can I speak to the manager?' I ask a smart, male assistant, and moan about our phone call, gruelling journey and the missing walking frame.

This assistant looks rather shifty.

'Are you pretending not to be the manager?' I ask. He owns up and dredges up a polite look of concern. I suspect it is a pretend one, used day after day on cross daughters and their elderly mothers who have fought their way here through crowds and traffic to try wheelchairs, frames and sticks that have disappeared.

Eventually we stagger out. I leave my mother sitting on some boxes of rubbish while I fetch the car. No other form of seating exists. Gone is her dream of the elegant tea in Sagné's. Anyway, it has long since been taken over and inferior gateaux are now served. I return to find her swaying in front of a smart antiques-shop window pretending she doesn't need a seat. Better to stand and suffer than to sit and be mistaken for an indigent.

At least she can use the relaxing luxury birthday footbath when she gets home: Wrong again. 'Do not use if your feet are swollen and you have varicose veins.' We are in for a jolly birthday.

WORMS

Some shocking news this week in our house. Gardener has got worms. How unfair. Of all the residents and visitors in our house, Gardener is the most hygienic. Over the years he has done his best to introduce a more scrupulous regime: no wet dishcloths in the sink, no licking spoons and putting them back in the pot, no uncovered food in the fridge, rubber gloves, masks and tongs must be used when handling poultry, and when eating out avoid mayonnaise like the plague.

For years I have slobbed about ignoring these rules, but it is Gardener who has the worms. Or perhaps we've all caught them. Panic stations. But every cloud has a silver lining. My mother has always resented Gardener's consumption of food, particularly cakes and ice-cream. She has often hidden her cakes away, forbidden him a single crumb, or perhaps grudgingly allowed him a mingy slice. Now she knows it wasn't greed. It was the worms. The poor fellow was ill.

But Rosemary takes a harsher line. 'I don't really want to hear about it,' says she strictly. 'Tiny children yes, but grown men, *no!*' The worms have opened the flood-gates and out pour all Rosemary's hidden feelings about Gardener, repressed until now because he is my friend.

'We're terribly unhygienic,' cries Rosemary, gathering momentum. 'You are disgusting. You fiddle with that dog, you pick up bits of fruit.' And still we don't get worms. To Rosemary this can only mean one thing. Gardener is dirty beyond measure. My mother shares this view. Just when Gardener had been found innocent of greed, he is now found guilty of filth. Never mind that nits, scabies, impetigo and worms can strike at random, regardless of class or level of dirt, or that scrabbling around in the earth in strange gardens might put him at extra risk. Say what I like, I cannot convince my mother or Rosemary otherwise. Gardener is a pariah – bringer of disease.

Luckily Gardener is unaware of all this. Fascinated by the complex lifestyle of the roundworm, he is busily telling everyone about its convoluted journey round his interior, which apparently began in March. 'The female roundworm,' says he proudly, 'lays a quarter of a million eggs a day!' Daughter runs screaming from the kitchen. And Gardener is planning to live here. He is off to a flying start.

SUPERSTITION – EVIL EYE

My mother comes home from her bridge game in a terrible flap. She is convinced that one of her acquaintances has cursed her. She does a mock spit and sticks her thumb between her fingers to ward off the spirits.

'She kept saying what a wonderful daughter I've got,' babbles my mother by way of an explanation.

'Isn't she just paying a compliment?' I ask.

'No!' roars my mother, stuffing her thumb through her fingers again in a panic. 'She's putting the evil eye on us! I know she is.'

What rubbish. It is 1998, but my mother thinks there is a witch at the bridge club. She must have caught this from my grandma, who also stuck her thumb between her fingers, spat *and* sewed bits of red ribbon on her underclothes, *and* made sure there were red garments in the window of her dress shop and would never allow my mother to sit on the table and swing her legs.

'Stop that,' Grandma would hiss in a fright. 'It means you're cursing your father and mother.' But perhaps my mother is right. Something odd is happening in our house. We are having terrible trouble with roast ducks. Crispy duck pancakes is the Daughter's favourite dinner, but every time we try and eat it, to celebrate something or other, everything goes horribly wrong. After all the fiddling about drying, marinading, roasting, and preparing, someone is bound to have a row or drama or tantrum, or is late, or feels suddenly and unaccountably sick, but whatever happens, somehow and for some reason, just when the duck is almost ready, the Daughter is bound to be in turmoil and cannot possibly eat.

So last time I pretended we weren't having one. 'What's for dinner?' asked the Daughter.

'Roast.'

'Roast what?'

'Roast meat.' Daughter guessed at once, ate a big sandwich because she was so hungry, then couldn't eat her duck, which naturally caused a row. But now I've done it again, because the Daughter's flying home from Amsterdam tomorrow and I thought it might be a nice welcome-home treat. What was I thinking of? Daughter is up in a plane and I buy a duck! So we ate it the night before her return home. Nothing went wrong.

SWEET LITTLE OLD LADIES?

One of my mother's favourite chums came to visit with her daughter. She is good-humoured, generous, calm, never involved in spats. What luck to have such a well-behaved mother! It's that *daughter* that's the problem.

The daughter looks pale, worn and grumpy. She comes into the kitchen for tea and explains herself. All is not as it seems. Her husband is off with another woman, her son has dropped out of college and when no one else is looking her mother is a tyrant. The daughter is desperate for some time off to see chums or read a gripping novel, just to take her mind off things but Mother won't allow it.

'You don't see that side of her,' moans the daughter. 'You should see her at home. She's always right. Even if she's wrong.' It's the *mother* that's the problem. I report back to my mother when the visitors have gone.

'You can't tell what anyone's like till you live with them,' says my mother ominously, and remembers her old friend Dora who had to come to England to have her teeth done because her cruel son wouldn't help her in France. What sort of a son was that? So Dora turned up at our house by surprise and ordered my father and mother to please find her a decent dentist, drive her backwards and forwards day after day for treatment and mince up all her food nicely. My mother phoned the son and begged him to come and remove his mother.

'Now you know,' said the son dismally, and took her away.

Meanwhile my friend Janet is sick of people praising her mother. 'Isn't she marvellous,' they say. 'What energy for eighty-eight! And she speaks so lucidly about world affairs!'

'That's because she's spent the last thirty years lying in a darkened room with a flannel over her forehead while her children and sainted husband scurry around dealing with life,' explains Janet rather bitterly. But some people must be what they seem. What about my mother's very best friend Eva with that tidy, kind and marvellous daughter?

'Oh, that's what *you* think!' I tell my mother. 'Eva's very stubborn. The daughter told me!'

'The bitch!' shouted my mother. 'Now let me tell you something. That daughter was so bloody tidy she'd have Hoovered Eva up if she'd had the chance. Would you believe it?'

Yes.

MONET

There is nothing like an outing to perk my mother up. Even if it turns out to be hell on earth, it's exciting to look forward to, otherwise my mother tends to sink into a glump in front of the telly. So Olga and I took her to the Monet exhibition. She is very fond of the Impressionists, especially the ones who paint flowers.

Of course this sort of outing isn't easy in a wheelchair, what with the heat, milling crowd and a broken lift in the Academy, but what use is an outing if one cannot moan about it afterwards? 'Make way for the cripple!' shouted my mother boldly, the crowds parted and there were the water lilies, and more water lilies, then another room full of water lilies.

'I've had enough bloody water lilies,' groaned my mother and turned to the willows and wisteria. But shouting didn't always clear the way. People bumbling round in headphones heard nothing, so after screaming 'Excuse me' a few times there was nothing for it but a sharp nudge in the ankles from a heavy metal wheelchair, and then we broke through, into the last room with huge paintings which one needs to see from a distance but can't because the crowds close in as you step back.

Still it made a change, and at least my mother's old chum from Hove met us in the marquee tea room afterwards. But what prices! 'One pound fifty for a drink of water!' roared my mother and her chum. 'Bloody disgrace!' And the tea! 'One pound for a paper cup of piss! Disgraceful!' And as for Olga's and my water-lily biros, we dared not reveal the price.

Then it was back through the crowds, traffic and fumes to our house to relax after all that excitement, but no chance. Just as I unloaded the shopping and my mother staggered from the car, our dog ran out of the house and spotted a chap parked in a gleaming people-carrier reading his paper with the window open. Keen to say hello, she jumped up to greet him, inadvertently clawing at the lovely new paintwork. Driver, a well-built fellow in the Grant Mitchell style, was understandably not pleased.

'That'll be a respray,' he growled. 'What you going to do about it?'

How's that for a day out?

MEAT MADNESS

Now that I have decided to be a proper vegetarian instead of nearly one, the whole household has gone mad for meat. They are suddenly into minced beef in a big way and all keen to cook spaghetti bolognese. And we only have one kitchen.

Our house is electric with clashing waves of envy and desire. Who will start the bolognese cooking? Who will dominate the kitchen area? Whose will taste the best? What luck that I am not involved in this and can just scurry up to my office with a cheese sandwich.

Meanwhile, Gardener has innocently got to the kitchen first. He is adhering more or less to an esteemed Italian recipe which takes four hours. This means sitting about in the kitchen to observe simmering and prevent sticking and burning. Meanwhile, up on the first mezzanine, my mother is also simmering, waiting to descend and cook mincemeat balls. In tomato sauce.

But wait. What's the matter with the Daughter? Up on the second floor she is in a white-hot fury, because for weeks she's been waiting to make a bolognese. I bought the mincemeat at her request, but then I forgot and promised it to my mother for the meat balls, meanwhile Gardener had whizzed out, suddenly enthusiastic, bought more stinky mincemeat and begun his sauce.

So we have layers of people stewing in various ways: waiting, cooking, seething. Downstairs Gardener cooks on dreamily, unaware of the furies upstairs. Once notified, he agrees to a postponement. His sauce will be frozen. Then we can have meat balls first, Daughter's bolognese second and Gardener's creation last. An endless run of minced corpse. And not only do I object on ethical grounds, but I never liked any of these dishes anyway.

I told my friends Toad and Nina about the mince problem, but to them spag bol is a dish from the distant past, when only foreigners ate garlic and no one went to Tuscany. But we are still back in the Dark Ages here with our cooking, battling with primitive rivalries: upstarts pushing the matriarch from her domain, a chap encroaching on women's territory, Daughter pitted against a usurper, and all to produce my least favourite meal, from meat into which shit has possibly seeped. I read about it in the newspaper.

So tomorrow it's my turn to carry on. Nut loaf for everybody.

STAFF

We now have a huge staff in our house, mainly appointed and needed by my mother: the homecare ladies to help with baths, the cleaning lady, physiotherapist, hairdresser, mobile-library lady and last week the builders as well for a mystery damp patch in the kitchen. The house is often mobbed with people.

Sometimes my mother is thrilled, but sometimes she is displeased. Obviously, with so many people in and out, some may not come up to scratch and there are bound to be mistakes made, so my mother keeps a sharp look out for anyone slacking. She is the Faultfinder General, patrolling the premises: that pan is not gleaming, this person is late, that person's tea break is too long, no one should be having a tea break anyway, that person has tramped mud, this fellow smells of smoke.

This morning I hear a roar of temper from the kitchen. A member of staff has used a two-cup tea bag in one cup and then *thrown it away*! My mother is incensed *and* her tea is too strong, *and* Hairdresser is two hours late! But why should Hairdresser hurry? She is agoraphobic and paid flumpence.

'Why not give her a bonus for arriving on time?' I beg my mother. Not a hope in hell. By her standards, *circa* 1950, Hairdresser's wages are reasonable. And now we need the windows cleaning. They have not been cleaned for six years and why not? The cleaners are too expensive, bound to be casing the joint and will return to rob us later. But I have found a new one, recommended by Rosemary.

'Only thirty pounds the whole house,' I shout. 'A bargain!'

'Daylight robbery,' shouts my mother.

Sometimes, when standards are unbearably low, my mother demands a sacking. And who is to do it? Me. But it's too late. Even if they were trailing filth through by the cartload or throwing tea bags away in handfuls I couldn't sack anyone, because by now I know all about them: the crack-addict son, the wastrel husband, the arthritis, holiday plans, vets' bills, financial struggle, high blood pressure, hopes and terrors.

So when my mother isn't looking I hand out extra wages, tea breaks, praises — anything to make working conditions here more bearable. It can't be too bad. No one has resigned yet. In one corner of north London, jobs are still for life.

HOLIDAYS

Rosemary and her sister are planning a heavenly trip to southern India and Tokyo to visit Rosemary's nephew and niece, who are doing noble works abroad. Easier said than done. It's cheaper to go backwards and forwards to London between stops than to do the round trip, Rosemary's messed up the booking and lost two deposits, *and* on Brother-in-law's credit card, Niece is in Kidnap Country, Nephew is running out of pocket money, Rosemary is running out of money altogether and worst of all, Niece has booked them into a Holiday Inn.

I thought their plans were too daring. I always find even a plain holiday more an ordeal than a pleasure and count the days until my return home. How many evenings running do you want to eat out, but why self-cater when you can do that at home? And what a strain it is to keep talking in a foreign language with a limited vocabulary, then get sunburn, or make sure you don't get sunburn, or drag round in the boiling heat staring at sights, when you could be relaxing in bed or your garden with a lovely book and ice-cream soda, just as if you were on holiday and for a fraction of the cost.

Luckily I can't go away anyway, because I can't leave my elderly dog and mother. They are the perfect excuse. But there is one small holiday that I fancy. I'd like to take my mother to Giverny for a last adventure while she can still move about. She longs to see it but doesn't dare. She's bound to drop dead or at least be very ill the minute we reach France, she just knows it. But I am suddenly determined. My cousin can come too and help push the wheelchair and I'm pretending I don't know that Monet's garden will be throbbing with crowds, so nothing can stop us. Anyway, why not be ill or die somewhere charming, rather than at home in the boring old bedroom?

Now all I have to do is call the French Tourist Office (at premium rate), French Railways, RADAR, find a hotel with a lift, work out dates, avoid bank holidays, fit in with Cousin, convince my mother, but still I'm ever so excited. First time for years. Until I tell Gardener my plan.

'You can get a video of Monet's garden,' says he. Oh, thank you.

TRAVELLERS

Daughter has returned home safely from Goa with a suitcase full of saris, but Rosemary and her sister are still out in India suffering from flu and holiday tummy, enduring intense heat and gruelling train journeys and trying not to fall out. I can understand the young going on adventurous holidays, but when one has varicose veins, a heart condition and sleep apnoea, why bother?

A poignant postcard arrived from Rosemary days ago, crammed with this ghastly news. After weeks of discomfort and no laughs, she had at last reached a heavenly seaside resort, but at what cost? Rosemary even mentioned 'going to the lavatory'. This is not a subject she usually alludes to, so things must have reached a critical level for her to have mentioned it on a postcard.

Naturally we are all worried. Yesterday her daughter rang in a panic. She had just spoken to Rosemary in Tokyo. 'She was in a very bad mood!' cried the daughter. 'She's running out of money, she's got a backache, she's having dizzy spells!' I ring Rosemary at once.

'What do you want?' she barks, not pleased at all. Shame. Here I am, ringing Tokyo, concerned and kindly offering to pick her up at the station but Rosemary is abusive. Something must be seriously wrong. If only she had stayed at home. The garden is heaven and she has completely missed her lilac. Personally, I am going right off holidays. The preparation is such a nightmare – all that packing, booking and worrying – that I am half dead before I leave.

But now our own tiny holiday is coming closer – three days in Giverny with my mother and cousin. We are terrified. My mother is frightened of dropping dead abroad, Cousin's knees won't bend properly and I'm frightened of driving, finding the way, going under the tunnel and my mother collapsing. And my leg hurts. Will I be able to drive at all?

Why am I putting us through all this? Because I still have a romantic notion that holidays can be fun and perhaps I need to go somewhere before agoraphobia sets in properly. My main worry, of course, is leaving the dog. I have been warned repeatedly. 'Get a dog and you'll never be able to go on holiday.' Exactly.

PASSPORT

My mother's passport has run out. What luck that I thought of it before we reached Dover. But how do I get her a new one? Can I collect it for her? I ring the passport office to find out. Fat chance. A robot woman answers. Press this button, press that button. Another robot voice. 'Press 2 for an operator.' Another robot. 'The system tends to be busiest on Monday mornings and mornings are busier than afternoons.' It is Thursday afternoon. I have a little scream. It gets me nowhere.

I am in for a six-hour wait at the passport office. And my mother must have a new ten-year passport, for a three-day visit to France. One-year visitors' passports are no longer available. She will now be able to travel abroad until she's 103. And we thought a united Europe would make life easier.

'Bloody ridiculous,' shouts my mother. 'I don't want to go.' Thank heavens she doesn't know the truth – £21 plus £10 handling charge for this special last-minute service. But we must go on our holiday. Everything is booked. We are locked into our plan. So off I go with my picnic, flask of coffee and Russian novel to the passport office. There is a scene from hell: milling crowds, hundreds of seats packed full, queues, wailing babies, bored children, breast-feeding mothers. I am number 485.

I moan on at the lady next to me about the silly ten-year passport. She insists that you don't need one for France. I'd better make sure. I join the mile-long queue for the one enquiry desk. Yes, we do need one. They may not look at it but she must have one. 'She might go on more holidays,' says the chap behind the counter. No, she won't. I'm having to drag her on this one. It will be my mother's Last Continental Holiday. A tragic look from this soft-hearted fellow. No one can bear the thought of last holidays. Why not? I'm looking forward to staying home when I'm ninety-three.

On Sunday we drove to my mother's friend Ruth's birthday in her son's divine wisteria-covered Surrey cottage. Perhaps three days here would have been more sensible. They have a lake covered in lilies, extensive gardens and a very attractive chicken called Janet. 'Giverny's very crowded,' says the son. 'You'll never get in.' Thank you.

GIVERNY

At last, after weeks of dread, we are off to Giverny. Luckily we have American Cousin with us. She has hired a swizzy car so we have room for our gammy legs, wheelchair, Zimmer, sack of pills and picnic. But what have we been worrying for? Le Shuttle is heaven. One minute we're in England, the next we're in France. My mother is thrilled. At the first snack stop she is able to talk loudly and fluently in French, her favourite hobby after bridge.

'It's so clean and tidy!' cries my mother as we travel along. The bridges are white and neat, the trees in lovely straight lines! 'The French are so *practique!*' roars my mother. 'Even the cows are clean!' Cream cows dot the green fields, the sun shines and before we know it we are at our hotel. All walls and ceilings are carpeted, rather like a glum brothel, but we love it. It is spotless, the breakfast divine, the proprietor charming, and there's lots more talking in French. 'No! My mother cannot be ninety-three! What excellent French, what an accent, what a vocabulary! We are on a talk marathon.

Next stop Giverny. Will it be the hell we have been promised? Luckily we have the wheelchair and American Cousin. With the help of both we jump the queue and enter Monet's famous garden, and there is still space enough between tourists to move. We are in luck. We shove my mother round the water garden, up, down and around the main garden, the crowds clearing as we approach, and what flowers!

Everything French, no cooking, no washing-up, no barking dog, just gazing and talking and now this — acres of fabulous flowers. And then we have our last supper. It is all exquisite: the fish soup, the ice-cream, the lemon pie. My mother has gone to heaven early. 'This is my swansong!' says she poignantly. 'No!' we all shout. 'It can't be.

Nobody's seen your new £31 passport yet.' We begged Passport Control at both ends to look but they couldn't be bothered.

So we've seen Giverny, we didn't get lost, drown in the tunnel, have an accident, become ill, drop dead, and here we are back in the Holloway Road, with its piles of crap, bursting rubbish bags and vile graffiti. Home again. We have survived our holiday. We even liked it.

UPSTAIRS DOWNSTAIRS

This morning I mixed up the dog's breakfast in our best wooden salad bowl by mistake. I forgot that the dog's bowl was still on the floor. I dare not tell anyone. They will start flapping about dog's germs. My mind is speeding up as it goes down the drain. Yesterday I had been up and down the stairs twenty-three times by 11 a.m. because I keep forgetting to take up what I went down for, then when I go downstairs for it again, the phone may ring or I may fancy a cup of tea and be distracted from my original mission, or not remember that I am on a mission, or I may remember it but pick up the wrong item by mistake, then get upstairs again and wonder why I've got it.

I am worn out with all this tramping up and down, especially with the torn ligament in my knee. But three doors along, Rosemary is doing the same. Ergonomically, our lives are fairly hopeless. Yesterday she went to the bottom of the garden to bring the washing in, was distracted by a beautiful rose, went back indoors to fetch the secateurs, but just then the phone rang, so she answered it, had a chat, went back upstairs, saw the ironing board, which reminded her of the washing, which was still at the bottom of the garden, and the whole thing started again.

Down she went to the kitchen, saw the secateurs, remembered the rose, picked lots of flowers, started arranging them, then realised that she was never going to have a clean, ironed shirt for work.

Luckily for her, no one was watching, but I have my mother anxiously on the look out for signs of dementia. She knows that if her primary carer goes round the twist, she is up the creek. And she often has her evening meal upstairs in bed, which means I am easily caught in the up-and-down amnesia routine. The difficulty here is getting all the items on the tray in one go. I am bound to forget one. 'Where's the mayonnaise/salt/horseradish?' asks my mother in a tragic way, because she doesn't really want to ask. Either way, someone loses out. She does without her mayonnaise, or I must go up and down the stairs again.

'Absent-minded professor,' wails my mother. Is it a compliment or not?

BATH TIME

It is several years since my mother has had a real bath. She can't get out of them. I used to haul her out once upon a time, but it was a dangerous manoeuvre, so we gave up. Since then she has a wooden plank and plastic seat arrangement, which is all right but nothing like wallowing in a proper, scented, soothing bath. Then a few weeks ago, she spotted these two very smart elderly women on telly in their black swimming costumes demonstrating Bathknight, a contraption which lowers you into your bath on a sling and then lifts you out of it. The answer to my mother's prayers.

Round came the salesman with half a pretend bath and demonstrated it in the living room. Salesman and my mother took turns trying the thing out. As Salesman's bottom was as fat as my mother's, they struck up a good rapport. My mother paid the deposit and ordered one.

But now three weeks have passed and delivery day has arrived. My mother wakes in a cold sweat. She has hardly slept. How could she? At 3 a.m. she awoke and realised that she was about to squander over a thousand pounds on something that is bound to electrocute her in the bath. And fancy believing a salesman! Madness! My mother is desperate to speak to someone who has used the thing and is not dead.

She rings Salesman in a panic. He puts her in touch with a woman who has used his product for ages and is still alive. My mother feels better. But I don't. I have a different secret worry. The contraption is to be fixed to the wall. Can our wall hold a thirteen-stone mother? It looks rather weedy since we pulled the ivy down. I imagine my mother crushed under a pile of rubble in her bath.

But it's too late. The wretched thing is on the way. It arrives. It is installed. We have another lesson, and then we're left alone to try it. The bath is filled, the machine hums and throbs, down goes my mother on her sling/electric chair into the foaming water of her first bubble bath for years. No electric shock, no collapsing house. It is heaven. Nothing has gone wrong. My mother even manages to relax. It is never too late for a new experience.

YEAR OF THE PENIS

I notice that people are bandying the word 'penis' about like never before and it isn't my favourite word. It sounds like something long, thin and pointy like a pencil, which isn't exactly what one is looking for, and that long *eee* makes it sound even thinner. 'Isn't that funny?' I said to Rosemary, 'whereas vagina has an open sound.'

'Stop it!' she shouted. 'You're entering a whole arena that I want nothing to do with.' And who can blame her. Contemplating male genitalia isn't everyone's cup of tea, but we must all do it, because this seems to be the Year of the Penis, what with the President waving his about, Viagra all over the place and the telly schedules stuffed with sex programmes.

Last week one could watch penises on telly for hours on end: pretend ones, real ones, inside and out, stuck with needles, measured, pumped up, stimulated and ready to go, or resting. 'Bloody disgraceful,' shouted my mother from her bedroom. Even with her sensitivities blunted by years of Kilroy, Vanessa and Jerry Springer, she was still shocked by the multitude of penises televised this week and the bold investigations into bodies, sex and odd behaviour: ladies with whips and bosoms pumped up almost to bursting, men crawling around swathed in rubber, bare people standing about, doctors and scientists measuring, testing and explaining *and* Monica's saucy reports.

On the positive side, flashers will rather lose their edge. We'll be so used to *those things* that they may as well brandish a corn on the cob. And this tidal wave of information might even act as a nationwide blanket contraceptive. Sexual overload and fatigue could set in. Years ago I saw an artistic Japanese film, *In the Realm of the Senses*, in which the protagonists were at it like knives for ages, until she chopped his penis off, although she adored it. Perhaps she was exhausted. We certainly were. Even though I removed my glasses, I still remember an endless blur of red and purple that made me feel quite ill.

Yesterday, for a change from the endless genitalia, Sylvia and I took the dogs for a walkie in the fresh air, but our heads were still swimming with penis thoughts from the week's telly. We climbed Kite Hill and gazed down at the London skyline, but it is now marred by large sticky-up buildings. Is there no escape?

GOODBYE SENSES

Sylvia's daughter entered the kitchen the other day and gave a cry of horror. Someone had made a vile smell. Of course it was the dog, but Sylvia hadn't smelt a thing. At seventy-six she is obviously losing another of her faculties.

'Something else to look forward to,' said the Daughter in a mocking way, and rushed out of the room holding her nose.

It would be easy to be downcast about this but I think Sylvia should be positive. The dog could be fainting in its own stench and Sylvia would be spared any unpleasantness. She could be imagining roses all the while. And look at these new scratch-and-sniff history books for children. Who wants to smell Henry VIII's gangrenous feet? Now Sylvia will be able to read these books to her great-nieces or possible future grandchildren in comfort. And as taste is 80 per cent smell, she will be able to eat up any old meal, however disgustingly cooked, and still smile appreciatively at the hostess.

Of course there are disadvantages. Her daughter has come rushing into the kitchen in a panic when the reek of escaped gas became overwhelming, but so far Sylvia has escaped unharmed. And she can't smell the lovely flowers in her garden. Last year she failed to smell the mahonia. Thinking there was something wrong with it, she added fertiliser rather lavishly and almost killed it. Just in time a friend smelt it and saved its life.

My mother, on the other hand, is often tormented by smell. 'I've got a very acute sense of smell,' she roars, glaring at the source of the tiniest hint of body odour, cigarette smoke or garlic. 'Who's been smoking/using the bathroom/frying fish?' she cries, rushing from her room with the air-freshener and spraying fiercely, clogging the house with a new stink and choking the dog.

All her life my mother has battled with smells: an uncle reeking of alcohol, visiting youths with smelly feet, colleagues with personal hygiene problems. Always she has spoken out boldly — advising, reprimanding and distributing Odorono roll-ons. Even now, sharp as ever and assailed by villainous stinks, my mother's nose gives her no respite. Our dustbins fester in the front garden, Gardener has sprinkled chicken shit in the back, visiting cats foul the borders and the dog has a recurrent bowel disorder. Life is far more relaxing for Sylvia, even if she can't wander about her garden dreamily sniffing at the azaleas and wisteria any more. Meanwhile I am getting more and more short-sighted. I must almost poke my nose into the dinner to see the bones in my fish. Is this another faculty on the way out?

GOODBYE DOG

Something very nasty has happened to the dog's pancreas. She must be given snacks every two hours and teaspoonfuls of honey when she feels faint. We know when she feels faint because her legs collapse. People are talking ominously about 'sensible decisions'.

We now have two old ladies staggering about the house. 'I wonder which of us will go first,' asks my mother. She often has a bet on this, but now the dog seems to have drawn the short straw.

'It'll only be about three or four weeks,' says Rosemary to my mother on the phone. My mother puts the phone down, looks at the beautiful brown dog and starts wailing. She is furious. What does Rosemary know? What do the vets bloody know? 'Nothing!' shouts my mother. This reminds her of her own very first infant boxer dog, which was given a death sentence by the vet but suddenly made a miraculous recovery. Perhaps the same thing will happen all over again. Meanwhile we are all fiddling around bursting into tears separately, looking desperately for signs of recovery.

In the morning the dog can scarcely lick honey from the spoon, but by lunchtime she's up barking for snacks and wagging her tail. At teatime she plays briefly with a cardboard box, in the evening she has breathing difficulties, exacerbated by the heat. I cram pills and sugar down her throat. Will she still be with us tomorrow? Every morning I expect a tragedy. Is she still breathing? Can she get up? And what about my mother? She's very quiet. Is she still with us? I have a quick inspection tour of the house. Everyone is still around.

But not for long. Rosemary was right. The poor dog's life is not worth living. She's stopped wagging her tail and given up on her favourite snacks. I have made the hideous sensible decision. We are off to the vet for the last time. Goodbye, lovely dog. Now I'm forever thinking she's in her bed waiting for a snack, or in her chair, or behind me in the car, or will be waiting when I come home or when I get up in the morning. But she isn't. The house is empty. Something enormous is missing. So far, no one has said, 'It was only a dog.'

NEW STAIRLIFT

The dreaded stairlift has broken down for the Nth time and my mother has been marooned upstairs, poaching in her bedroom in the broiling heat. Along comes the stairlift man but he can't mend it.

'Never seen one like this before,' says he in a sullen mood, fiddles about for an hour and a half, fails to mend it and leaves. A seventy pound fee. Another man calls, another call-out charge. He mends it, but only for a week. Time for a new stairlift. What a grisly prospect: queues of stairlift salesmen, hours of staring, paying attention and deciding, spending thousands of pounds.

But luckily my mother's attitude to money has changed. She now knows that saving money gets you nowhere. It will either be frittered by your granddaughter or daughter or the hordes of spongers and mendicants waiting in the wings, or wasted on nursing homes, home helps and aids that she would have got for nothing if she hadn't saved her money. So wow! Let's go for the squillion-pound state-of-the-art stairlift.

Round comes the first stairlift salesman. His stairlift sounds heavenly: tasteful, extra bar to stop you falling downstairs, battery, remote control and no noise. Ours, when functioning, sounds like a First World War tank. But we are still cautious. 'Beware of thieves and rascals who will always surround you!' my father used to say, and he was right. Salesman endorses his opinion. Stairlifts are now a growth industry peppered with crooks.

'Remember,' says Salesman poignantly, 'it could easily be the last expensive thing that someone buys.' What a sour farewell to this world, to be ripped off at the last. Then he tells us a cautionary tale, about the lady who bought a £5000 stairlift from another company. They promised to buy it back if necessary. Three months later she moved into a bungalow and they bought it back — for £280. And charged £350 to remove it.

My mother may be mellowing out, but she still wishes to spend her money properly rather than throw it down the drain and is keen to know which company will buy our stairlift back if she drops dead soon after installation, or in a few months or years? We ask all the stairlift men this question. Only one gives a precise answer. We choose his stairlift, but is he fibbing? Watch this space.

WORRYING PROSPECTS

On Sunday Rosemary visited her elderly Auntie Mary in hospital. Auntie was cleaning her teeth. She spat into the tooth mug because there was no alternative.

'Naughty Mary,' said the nurse strictly, tapping her on the hand.

'I'm so sorry,' said Auntie, 'but I wanted to say thank you to my niece for so kindly visiting . . . ' but the nurse had gone, off to the other side of the ward, too busy for a long polite sentence, and never heard the explanation. Rosemary found this very depressing. There was her aunt, former Head of the Royal College of ****, being ticked off like a witless baby.

'I'm haunted by the helplessness of old age,' said Rosemary, looking desolate. No wonder. Last night, at home alone, her children all away, Rosemary bleached the sink in an efficient way and went up to bed. She awoke this morning to find the kitchen awash, floating slippers and a paddling cat. She had left the tap on all night.

'I can't live alone!' cried Rosemary, thinking of her future and her auntie. And then there was another red alert. My mother had left a desperate gabbled message on her answerphone.

'Where are you?' wailed my mother's voice. 'I don't know where Michele is! The AA man can't find her.' Home alone, my mother naturally assumed that I was dead, crashed en route to my broken-down car. Then hot on the heels of my mother's message came another from Arthur, another elderly chum of Rosemary's. His wife had disappeared. Where could she be? She'd been gone all day and he was too poorly to cook his own dinner. So was my mother. Rosemary was surrounded by helpless elderly persons asking for assistance. Meanwhile, her cork tiles had all come loose and were curling up at the edges and Rosemary had tripped over several and broken bits off.

Her kitchen looked like a slum, and she had been hoping to sell her house. Who would buy it now? Left alone for one night, Rosemary had wrecked her kitchen, and she is only sixty.

I find Rosemary standing on the pavement looking rather pale. 'Your mother's been phoning, Arthur's been phoning, everybody's worried about everybody.' And now I am worried about Rosemary. So we have a worriers' support network. In an odd way, this rather cheered us up.

NEW DOG

We have a new dog. Daughter and I take it for a first walk, but we keep bumping into all the dog walkers who remember the old dog. They offer condolences along with congratulations for the new baby. I spend the walk blubbing and thinking of the last dog's lovely old face. It hovers like a saint in the background. And our new puppy is flawed. It has fleas, worms, its teeth are frightfully undershot and it's a nervous wreck. And it has no tail. For years I have vowed never to have another dog without a tail, and now I have one. I couldn't find any with tails quickly enough. So on top of all its other problems, it's an amputee.

Oddly enough these problems seem to be a good thing. We are so busy fussing over our new dog that it takes my mind off the old dog, who is still in a black box on a bookshelf in my bedroom. My plan was to sprinkle her over our favourite bits of Heath. Then in the spring, up would come the bluebells, marguerites and wavy grasses – a sort of secular reincarnation, but I can't do it. I can hardly look at the box and I can't face the sprinkling.

Meanwhile, our new dog needs intensive care. It is thin as a rake, cringing and frightened of everything and everyone, except the Daughter and me. It will hardly eat or drink, it won't go in and out of doors, we can't tempt it anywhere because it doesn't want a biscuit. We have never seen such a weedy boxer. It has lived for four months in country kennels and is now having tremendous difficulty adapting to a house in town.

Will it/she adapt to the Heath? Will she get on with Sylvia's dog – my old dog's best friend – or will they fight and ruin our walks? I take her for the first meeting. Luckily our dogs are mad keen on each other. What a relief. They carry on where the old dog left off – same games, same pouncing, same hide-and-seek, only now Sylvia's dog is the grown-up. Our new dog is bolder and lovelier by the minute, I have stopped blubbing, go for regular walkies and talk about dogs again. Rosemary is sick to death of it already. Thank goodness things are returning to normal.

WESTMINSTER PARKING

It is bad for my mother to be stuck too long in her roasting bedroom with the fan-heater and telly roaring on, so we planned an exhilarating outing into town. What luck that we have an orange disabled badge but what a horrid shock to find a ticket stuck on the car. Whatever for? There is the warden, only yards away. I demand an explanation.

'You've been there more than an hour,' lies the warden. I have not. I can prove it. There is the orange badge truthfully indicating our time of arrival.

'Did you put money in first?' he asks, just managing not to smirk. It is difficult, when one is in a raging temper, to spot a trick question. No, I answer. That was my big mistake. I had forgotten that we were in Westminster where normal rules do not apply. Here you must pay the minimum fee, then you can stay for an hour. Be warned. This is a secret until you get caught and punished, or unless you've read your disabled-parking booklet carefully, phoned up the Westminster disabled parking number and found out what the rules are. But you can't because this number actually has nothing to do with disabled parking. It's only for paying fines or having clamps removed. Otherwise, all the operators are busy, please try later.

I have a scream at the warden. He has ruined our outing. My mother stands pale and trembling, clutching her Zimmer on the pavement. And she has forgotten her angina spray.

We drive round the corner to Cousin's flat. But dare we park on a yellow line with our useless badge? I jump out, ring Cousin's bell, screech at her to come downstairs, because here comes the warden again, searching for cripples to persecute. I run and ask him if I may park on a yellow line.

'No. Park in a bay,' says he. There isn't one. What am I meant to do with my collapsing ninety-three-year-old mother? She did want to visit Cousin for a cup of tea, but she can't. I have another scream and drive round in circles waiting for Cousin. Warden couldn't care diddly-squat. He is on a roll. Last week I heard that Westminster raked in £39 million from parking fines, more than any other borough. Now we know how they do it.

NOISE NUISANCE

As I grow older I long for extensive periods of absolute silence. There is no such thing where I live. One can only experience calm wearing ear-plugs and heavily sedated.

Last Saturday I was woken at 3 a.m. from a divine sleep by my mother honking her emergency hooter. Was it a robber or a heart attack? I staggered to her bedroom and there she was at the open window, hooting wildly into the night air. She had been driven to the borders of madness by a party raging behind our house and thought, in her crazed, exhausted state, that they might hear her hooter, realise how annoying they were and shut up.

We phoned the Town Hall to alert the noise officers, but lucky them, they go home to bed at 3 a.m. At least my mother sleeps at the back of the house. Stuck at the front I am woken every hour or so by people wandering up and down the street at all hours, carousing, arguing and laughing loudly as if it were lunchtime. I would like to rush out there, hold them up at gunpoint and place them in the stocks, gagged, until morning.

Nor can one rest during the day, what with the odd car alarm going off at dawn, thunderous pop music blaring from windows, the house shaken and blasted by passing cars throbbing with noise, Rosemary's Perfect Son practising his drumming and the Daughter and her chums galloping up and down the stairs relentlessly.

And because of the heat we must all have our windows open while the noise of enervated families shrieking within pours out and annoys all the other boiling and exhausted families who are trying to control themselves.

But it isn't just the hot weather. I suspect that the world is growing generally noisier and many of the public are partially deaf. Last night Daughter and I went out to dinner in a restaurant of her choice. Over the thunderous pop music, waitresses shouted cheerfully and Daughter and I lipread or roared at each other in order to converse. Being one of the new hearing-impaired generation, her ears terminally damaged and senses banged flat by clubbing and very loud music, the Daughter thought this a relaxing venue. Why was I scowling?

We had an uninhibited row about it. Luckily no one could hear us.

MOUNT VESUVIUS

About 280 years ago, Lord Hervey had trouble with his mother. He called her Mount Vesuvius, because 'from her mouth poured fire and rubbish'. I must say I sympathise. My mother erupted last week. Yet again she has turned against Rosemary. At the sound of the R-word, out pours a molten flow of bitterness-speak. It is difficult, under these conditions, to invite Rosemary round for tea, so I have taken to visiting her in her small apartment.

'Where are you going?' roars my mother.

'Out!' I am fifteen again. I cannot say R . . . and risk another tremor.

But on Saturday Rosemary braved it. Down in the kitchen we were out of the glare of my mother's fury. But Rosemary is not one to cower or suck up. She too likes to express her opinions in a loud, clear voice. And both she and my mother are highly skilled grudge-bearers. The air prickled with hatred.

Rosemary and I battled on with our coffee break. No sound came from my mother's room. Did she know I had a visitor or was Rosemary's voice drowned out by the sound of *The Waltons* on telly? I do hope so. Rosemary's remarks were rather inflammatory and if my mother had come belting out of her room to retaliate there could have been clashing antlers and blood on the walls.

What a sorry situation. Here I am, nearing sixty, and still barely able to invite my chums round to tea without my mummy's approval. Rosemary is not the only one. Over the years many of them have blotted their copybooks somehow. Some ate too much dinner, some didn't wash up, some answered back, some wore horrid clothes, some were rowdy and worst of all, some have *taken advantage*. Only a very few have spotless records.

But as I like to assert that I am a grown-up, I press on, entertaining chums regardless, although the mood in our house is not always as mellow as I would like. I party on a knife edge. Will there be sulks, glares, insults, a fight? Then gradually the temperature cools. Life simmers along. And there is at least one thing about living here in Temper Towers that my mother appreciates. It is rarely dull.

HOME ALONE

My mother has been feeling ill and weedy lately, so she's given me repeat instructions about her funeral, which she assumes is imminent. To make sure I get it right, she's told Rosemary and Gardener her plans as well. 'You're to have me cremated here, drive me to Hove and sprinkle me over Grandpa [my father] and then you're to have a party,' says she bravely.

At least my mother knows that when she drops dead someone is bound to notice and a fuss and the planned funeral will follow. She is in luck. I hear that scores of elderly persons are apparently dropping dead at home and rotting away undiscovered for months. Perhaps they're home alone because the hospitals are busting at the seams and having to shove the elderly out rather more quickly than they would like.

My friend Harriet's mother has been sent home dementing with a broken collar bone, she won't take her antibiotics, watches only *Teletubbies* and feeds her meals-on-wheels to the badgers. But my friend Caroline's father, eighty-eight, after several strokes and a kidney infection, never even got to hospital in the first place. It was full up. For a couple of heavenly weeks nurses were sent to his home day and night. Then the night care stopped, leaving his eighty-five-year-old wife to carry him to the lavatory four times a night.

Now Rosemary's eighty-seven-year old auntie has been knocked down and squeezed into hospital, where the doctor and nurse had a squabble, in front of Rosemary, about whether to give Auntie antibiotics or not. One of those handy chest infections had come along to clear out some geriatrics. Luckily the nurse won and Auntie got her antibiotics. Soon Auntie can be shoved off home. But then what? Caroline is shelling out £90 a night for private carers. Harriet has a bargain, at £350 a week.

It's that or give up your job, home and family and move in with the elderly parent. Or move them in with you. Now that most of us are over sixty and the National Health is not a magic porridge pot, the extended family may soon be compulsory again. There are benefits. It is rarely boring and relatively economical. We have had a reprieve. My mother is only anaemic. She is now guzzling watercress like a starving horse. Funeral plans are on hold again.

FADING FAST

4 a.m. My mother's emergency hooter goes off. She has an ominous pain in her chest. What is it? Indigestion? She's pulled a muscle trying to shut the sash window? Or heart attack? We run through the possibilities.

'Take my rings!' cries my mother in the usual way, preparing for hospital and worse. Shall we shoot off to A&E? 'Wait a bit,' croaks my mother, and tries the angina spray, the peppermint tea, the painkiller and the hot water bottle. One of them works. The pain subsides. And it is almost 4.44 a.m., the witching hour. My father's favourite number and a cluster of fours coinciding with chest pain means, in my mother's book, that he is probably hovering around accompanied by the Reaper, ready to escort her to Elsewhere.

No wonder we are on double red alert. But it was just another false alarm. At dawn my mother is still with us. She calls Jenny, the homeopath/acupuncture/osteopath lady who speeds round, wrenches her about rather cleverly and improves things. It was a digestive problem.

My mother perks up. Her digestion improves. Then her chest nearly packs in. She can't breathe properly. 'One bloody thing after another,' she croaks. 'I'm fading fast!' We call the doctor. My mother has gone meek and quiet. This throws me into a panic. Something must be seriously wrong. It is. She has a chest infection and it's her birthday on Saturday – ninety-four. Will she make it?

Yes. We take her to a Chinese restaurant where the elderly are treated with reverence. We know because we've taken her there before. Again she is showered with praise, presents, congratulations and then presented with a toffee-banana birthday cake. Staff are queuing up to give her a kiss. Perhaps we should all retire to China,

117

where the elderly are considered wise and wonderful rather than a mouldering burden. Just one evening of it, plus antibiotics, has reclaimed my mother from the jaws of death.

But it was only a brief reprieve. Days later my mother is hooting again. The chest pains again. 'I wish someone would come and shoot me!' she croaks. Who can blame her? We call Jenny again, another improvement and reprieve. On Saturday we are meant to be going to another party. Will we make it this time? No wonder my mother is browned off. I mention her condition to Sylvia on our dog walk.

'I wouldn't mind dying tomorrow,' says Sylvia cheerily. She is in her late seventies, still striding about with the dog and getting excited about football matches. I thought she was having a good time. 'Not really,' says Sylvia. 'and it's only going to get worse.'

POLITELY STARVING

On Wednesday I drove my mother to her distant bridge club, wrecking my day. I am prepared to drive for hours out into the backwoods because my mother is desperate for an outing. One more day stuck in the house and she will blow a fuse. I drive home, then back to get her and then back home again. I am a real saint.

'Did you have a good time?' I ask my mother on our return.

'No!' she shouts. 'That X gets on my bloody nerves!' Why did I bother with the marathon drive? Why is my mother not grateful and polite, like Rosemary's auntie? Auntie would never dream of criticising anyone or anything in such a way. Last month she was grateful and polite in hospital. Unfortunately, she couldn't stretch her injured arm out, reach her food or get it into her mouth, but she was much too polite to bother the nurses. Rosemary was worried she might starve to death in there.

'Why don't *you* feed her?' I asked. 'Because Auntie doesn't want to be spoonfed,' said Rosemary. 'It's too humiliating.' At least that's what everybody thought Auntie thought. Rosemary and all the other visitors and relatives were too polite to shove spoonfuls of dinner into Auntie's mouth, the nurses weren't spooning in dinner because they didn't have time and nobody asked them to, and if they asked Auntie why she'd hardly eaten a crumb, she would say very politely that she'd had quite enough, thank you.

Why couldn't everyone be more forthright? Perhaps my mother's method has something to be said for it. I'm beginning to feel like my mother. I want to rush up to the hospital with a big bowl of delicious and nourishing stew, waft it under Auntie's nose and say, 'Now look here, Auntie, we know you can't reach your dinner and you're embarrassed about being spoonfed, but it's only till your arm's better, so get this down you!'

Rosemary wouldn't dare speak to her auntie like that, but I think I know someone who could manage it. It's about time my mother had another outing.

BOYFRIENDS

It is sometimes difficult for a mother to appreciate the qualities of her daughter's friends, especially if they are male. My daughter and I are visited by chaps, but they rarely come up to my mother's standards.

'There must be something nice about him *if you say so*,' says she bitterly. 'I'd better not say anything. *I might say too much*.' She has occasionally refrained from overt criticism, but my visiting chap has only been allowed a small portion of cheesecake. Daughter's boyfriend was allowed none at all. There are ways and ways of expressing an opinion.

Some mothers, even though they loathe these fellows, are able to conceal their feelings, but my mother cannot. Try as she might, waves of hatred swirl about the house, her revulsion is supressed, but for how long? Often hints of it seep out – a tiny barbed remark, a sulk, a Rosa Klebb look. These are warning rumbles before the explosion of murderous criticism that usually erupts in the kitchen, epicentre of conflict.

Naturally a mother wishes to protect her child from scoundrels and advantage-takers. My mother can spot one a mile off. So zealous is she that sometimes the innocent are falsely accused. Yesterday Rosemary came over for a spoonful of mayonnaise and my mother flashed on to red alert. Unknown to her I had borrowed Rosemary's eggs earlier that day.

'I'd like you to know that this is reciprocal!' cried Rosemary, fearfully offended. But usually there is no trial or opportunity for defence. My mother does not take prisoners. One misdemeanour, one helping of ice-cream too many, one lot of washing-up not done, then the culprit is judged, condemned and never forgiven. Daughter's friend helped himself to toast without asking, my friend grabbed for extra chocolate cake, and now it is all over for them.

This does not help when one is trying to conduct a romance, but my mother has been trained from infancy to be on the lookout for spongers. Her own mother fought tooth and nail to banish my father, but fortunately failed. Still my mother presses on.

'Please, Rosemary,' she begged poignantly, 'grant me this one wish as a dying woman!'

'Of course!' said Rosemary in a fright. 'Whatever is it?'

'DON'T LET HER MARRY HIM!' What a burden for Rosemary! Only she could save my mother from the eternal torment of knowing that a parasite may deprive me of all my worldly goods. And I thought you could stop worrying about daughters straight after A-levels.

CLEANING LADY TROUBLES

Every now and again, the cleaning lady problem erupts. My mother or daughter suddenly become discontented with Kathy the cleaning lady and orders me to find someone more efficient. I absolutely cannot do this. After three years I am now friends with Kathy, we are *au fait* with each other's personal problems, I know all about her difficult son, that annoying fellow who won't leave her alone and her endless battle over the central heating and there is no possible way I could sack Kathy.

My daughter and mother cannot get to grips with this. They see the dust nestling on surfaces and blinds, the spiders' webs draped about, the grunty carpet corners that are never Hoovered, the crockery piled in all the wrong places and these little things grate on their nerves.

'What would you do if I said I'd found a really excellent cleaning lady who could start tomorrow,' snaps Daughter, with a fierce glint in her eye.

'I do not wish to discuss this. I cannot sack Kathy.' 'Why not?/Because./Because what?/Because I like her./Why do you like her?' On and on goes the Daughter like a hornet. She doesn't understand that Kathy is nervous, dare not move things in case she breaks, mislays or muddles them up, which means she can't clear any surfaces, which means that the surfaces cannot be cleansed.

This suits me. I don't want a strange and bossy person stacking up my papers or throwing away vital scraps and bits by mistake. Much better to have a light layer of dirt and refuse about. At least the rising tide of filth in the kitchen is kept at bay and central areas Hoovered, by Kathy. And very important — Kathy and the dog love each other.

In a fury, Daughter whirls round the house like a tornado clearing surfaces. This is fabulous. Now Kathy can clean them without fear. But Daughter is still not satisfied. She leaves a bossy list of tasks to be done. She was born to rule, like her grandma. 'Why can't I have the job?' asks Daughter fiercely.

She can. Then we shall have an extra super-efficient cleaning lady for free. Marvellous. There's only one snag. Daughter won't be around for long. Soon she'll be off, on holiday, or back to university. Kathy, on the other hand, isn't going anywhere. Ever.

PNEUMONIA

My mother has had pneumonia. I dragged her to the doctor, who rang the hospital, found her a bed and sent us straight there. But my poor mother still had to sit in casualty for hours on end. Silly innocents. We though you just trotted off to hospital with your suitcase and got into bed. Wrong. First of all you have to go through A&E, sit on metal seats and wait among the moaning crowds, wailing infants, roaring drunks and blaring telly, even if you are ninety-four, can't breathe and are practically flaking out on your chair.

So my mother sat wilting while I flapped around trying to hurry things up. It did us no good. It is the hospital doctors, not your GP, who decide whether or not you may have a bed. This was a grisly experience. I have already had one parent die on a hospital trolley and am not keen to have it happen again. But even a trolley is better than a metal chair and after an hour or so, my mother was lying down on one somewhere quiet. Tea and sandwiches were brought round, doctors and nurses were perfect. 'Very thorough!' croaked my mother and eventually, five hours later, she was trundled off to a proper bed, then the next day, off to the women's geriatric ward.

'Where's the red carpet?' she asked on arrival. Soon she was gaining strength and able to carry out lavatory inspections. Within hours she had found out which ladies left the lavatories spotless and charmingly perfumed and begun to time her visits to follow them. Then there were menus to tick, pills to take, oxygen up your nose, cheery nurses backwards and forwards. My mother's breathing and appetite improved, the hairdresser was booked and things were definitely looking up, until the poor lady in the next bed died in the night.

My mother lay there, feet away, listening to the awful sounds of the Reaper so close by. She didn't have much of a sleep and looked rather pasty the next day. This close encounter did her appetite and breathing no good at all, but she is still improving. A new lady has moved into the empty bed. 'Life goes on,' says my mother with a grim look. And luckily so does hers. She will be home next week.

THROWAWAYSIES

Rosemary has sold her house. We wish she hadn't. Her living room is full of boxes of belongings, Rosemary keeps bursting into tears and I'm pretending she's just going on holiday. How are we to manage? Who will we borrow a carrot from? Who will we shout and moan at? Who will we run to when we need to escape our homes for ten minutes? Worse still, Rosemary hasn't found a new house yet and must stay with her auntie and put everything into storage, which costs a fortune. So she must do some strict throwing away. Her daughters are sweeping through the basement like an enema and hurling objects on to the pavement, starting with my old bicycle. I lent it to them years ago and now it's out on the street. Without my permission.

'Do you want it back?' asks Rosemary. I'm not sure. I go indoors for a think. I hate cycling, it gives me leg-ache and asthma, but suppose the car breaks down or world petrol supplies dry up? I may *have* to ride it one day. But I have nowhere to put it. The new cooker and dryer are blocking the hall, Daughter's computer and washing are stuck in the living room and the cellar is stuffed with Gardener's boxes. I ring Rosemary and order her to take my bicycle in again, but too late. Someone has made off with it.

I dare not tell my mother. Rosemary will become hate figure of the month yet again for wasting my bicycle. My mother has not yet come to terms with the throw-away culture. She lovingly washes and reuses her social services disposable knickers and in our house a J-cloth is for ever. I suspect I am taking after her. The house is stuffed with things that I can't throw away: dead plants, old sewing machines, a stick of rock, dull books, worn-out sheets. Who knows? The plants may return to life, I may eat the rock or mend the sheets with my machine. Perhaps I need to move. Then I shall *have* to throw away rubbish. Any houses going in Rosemary's auntie's street?

PERSONALISED WHEELCHAIR

My mother was most discontented with her last wheelchair outing. It gave her a dreadful hip-ache for weeks. But now she is to have a new one specially fitted at the wheelchair centre.

What a dreary venue. Portraits of elderly ladies accompanied by the odd saintly carer line the walls. The artist has done his/her level best to make these old ladies look sweet, contented and attractive, but my mother is sickened.

'Yech,' she groans. 'I hope I don't bloody look like that.' However, the ladies in the fitting room are charming. They are kind, attentive and cheery, measure my mother's legs, laugh at her jokes and one of them has exactly the sort of jumper that my mother has always longed for. She would like to spend a week here being pandered to.

I whizz my mother up the corridor in her new chair for a try-out, past scores of drear paintings of little old ladies. We battle with depression. These portraits are not uplifting. Luckily my mother is able to express her opinions forcefully back in the fitting rooms.

Within a couple of days the gleaming new wheelchair arrives. I take my mother out for a ride to a local park. Sensibly we have two extra attendants. The new luxury-fitted wheelchair is still hell to push. Even a half-inch kerb is a major obstacle when one has a thirrteen-stone mother in the chair. And this is central London where motorists are not keen on waiting patiently for the infirm to get out of the road. They roar past missing us by a whisker while we fiddle at the kerbside. It takes two to tip the wheelchair from the back and one to pull it up from the front.

This was a hair-raising ride for my mother, what with the chair going wild round sloping corners, like a renegade supermarket trolley. All three of us are half dead after our little walk, even with my mother getting out at steep kerbs and staggering across roads. What if she were unable to walk at all?

And it isn't just the practical problems. Having once been pushed round myself in a chair with a nearly broken ankle, I notice that the walking public are fairly badly behaved. They do not get out of the way when they spot a wheelchair coming, but tend to stand blocking paths and staring in a dull way.

At least we have no problems at present. It is freezing cold and my mother does not wish to go out in her lovely new wheelchair. It stands neglected, blocking the hall until spring.

THE WICKED STAIRLIFT

Over the past few months our stairlift has been playing up. Screws have dropped off and disappeared, bits have come loose, it has had odd moods, starting only when jiggled, and just before Xmas it stopped altogether.

Ages ago, at the loss of the first screw, we had called for help. Weeks later a man appeared. He dashed in, looked and was gone in a microsecond. What more could he do? He didn't have the right screws. A thirty-pound call out charge. He would come back and repair the stairlift, for another call out charge, plus mending charge, when, and only when, we had paid the first call out charge.

The stairlift people are on to a winner here. They may charge what they like for as little as they like, because when you have a large and angry mother trapped on the first floor waiting for the stairlift to release her, they have you over a barrel.

Naturally we put up a fight. Why should we pay for some ill-equipped fellow to do nothing? But it took him half an hour to drive here, so he had to be paid. Or else. We paid up. Back he came, with an accomplice. My mother didn't recognise him.

'Are you that bugger that ran in and out last time?' she roared from the landing. 'Bloody cheek! Thirty pounds for nothing!'

'Not me, madam,' he lied, then he told us a secret. 'You can have a complete service, including call-out, for fifty-five.'

This was news to us. What a pity we hadn't been told this in the first place. We had the service. The stairlift was mended. My mother burst out of prison to play bridge. She enjoyed another week of freedom, then just before New Year, the stairlift broke down again. All its lights went out. This time my mother was marooned downstairs, twelve steep steps away from the bathroom and lavatory. She crawled upstairs on her knees in a raging temper, cursing the hated stairlift.

I called for help again. A polite and patient man answered. He would come the next morning. And he did, equipped with the right tools, mended the stairlift, explained its workings and left us in heaven. Until the next bill arrives. Perhaps cabinet ministers considering disability allowances might remember our little adventures with the stairlift. Good job we could afford them. But what if we couldn't?

BIG SHOES

My mother has big, red, shiny, burning feet. She's had them for ages but no one has a remedy. Why? Because it's old age. Her feet have had it. So she's forever moaning and dabbing at them, rubbing ointment on, weeping or having a shout, while the feet torment her through the night.

I see my future here. Last week I tried the Christmas shopping. I set out in a cheery and optimistic mood but after two hours clomping along, my feet were broiling, throbbing stumps. I had a cry and came home. Present-less. I have my mother's feet, but bigger.

Sometimes I try to ignore the hereditary foot problem. Last year I bought eight pairs of fashionable shoes at once. This may sound extravagant, but when one is Mrs Freak with size 9½B feet, it is a stroke of luck if you can even find one clodding pair to fit. And Daughter was egging me on. She has always longed for an elegant mother, clip-clopping along in swizzy high heels, and this was her chance to have one. During our buying frenzy, we imagined that I might wear these things. I even had a party to go to at the weekend – Daughter's twenty-first. So I wore my new high heels. Next day I had foot, waist, back and almost whole body ache.

Now it's party time and out come the high heels again. I've been to two parties so far this year wearing flat shoes and have been harshly criticised, by close friends, on both occasions. What good is a ravishing new frock, striking new hairdo, fabulous jewellery and the top looking like a Christmas tree, if the feet are a frumpy let down? And anyway, this year, very high heels are a must, so perhaps those heels are worth all the pain. Not only do they enhance any leg, but they do odd things to your bottom, back and front. Apparently this is another plus. I read it in the Sunday papers.

Luckily there was a party just round the corner. Near enough to clop round in the pig's-trotter heels, clop home again mid-party, give my mother her baked potato, take off the crippling stilt heels and run back again to the party. I left the shoes in the hall. With any luck the dog will eat them.

MILLENNIUM PARTIES

My friend Virginia is in a dreadful flap over millennium parties. She's been invited to three already and doesn't really want to go to any of them. People are pressuring her like anything to go to *their* party, but whatever she does she's going to put at least two people's noses out of joint. New Year's bad enough but this is a thousand times worse. It's this year that you really know who your friends are.

So no one can decide whose party to go to and anyway they're all waiting to see if they get a better offer, so they can't accept any invitations yet, which means that nobody can organise their party properly because no one will tell them for certain whether they're coming or not. But the trouble with millennium parties is that as everyone's having one you have to book the venue early, but you can't because you don't know how many are coming and the venues probably cost an arm and a leg and who wants to waste a fortune on a load of worthless friends who are being sniffy about your party?

Come the millennium then, lots of us are going to be stumping round in a sulk because our friends have spurned us on the most important evening for centuries and the new century will be off to a buttocky start.

What luck then to have an elderly mother and be able to pull out of this ghastly scrum. For once Virginia is thrilled that her mother is throwing a party. It is her perfect excuse And mine. How can one leave one's elderly mother alone on the eve of a new century? Nor can I take mine anywhere because she's much too feeble to withstand a big noisy party or to stay up till midnight.

We can all stay in, which is what we're longing to do anyway. And it's not our millennium. We're not even Christian. Sylvia is planning to send Chinese New Year cards to all her friends so they know just what to expect. In the meantime I told Virginia that if she doesn't go anywhere and she needs a break from her mother's party at the last minute, then she can always come to our house, because we're bound to be in.

She'd better bloody well turn up.

FORTH BRIDGE

One ghastly truth has emerged over the past month. I now know that nearly every house in our street and the surrounding neighbourhood is cleaner, tidier, more tasteful and more comfortable than ours. Even the dogs and cats are neater and odourless.

I know this because we visited extensively over the festive season and worse still, my mother knows too, because I trundled her about partying. A new world opened to my mother – a clean, smart world of spacious living rooms, fabulous kitchen extensions, charming neighbours, divine snacks and buffets. Naturally, on our return home she began to compare and contrast. Why did our home look like a dark and tiny slum and everyone else's like a large, airy mansion, if all the houses were exactly the same size?

Last week, while dining out across the road, I met a lady who knew my mother, so I recklessly whizzed her over to our house to visit. My mother was overjoyed, or would have been, if the surprise visit hadn't been tarnished by shame. I'd forgotten that the visitor would see our interior: the cracked paintwork, the washing dangling from radiators, the rumpled throws, the scattered dog chewies.

Who would guess that I devote much of my life to cleaning this Forth Bridge of a house but getting nowhere? I finish the kitchen, the lounge looks a tip, I tidy the lounge, the bathroom is a swamp, I clean the bathroom and bedrooms, the kitchen is a slum again, the fridge stinking, the sink clogged, the bin choc-a-bloc. Where does all the filth and debris come from?

Until recently I have had Rosemary nearby in another slum for consolation. Neither of us could conquer the housework. We would stare across the road together, united by domestic failure, looking enviously at the smart houses opposite. But now I am on my own.

Rosemary has moved away into her new flat. I dragged my mother there for a party. She inspected the new premises thoroughly. 'I can't fault it!' she cried.

What a surprise! My mother can usually find fault if she searches carefully, but not this time. Rosemary's flat was perfection: lovely new kitchen, no stairs, filth or clutter, not even a cat. But perhaps one day, when her children come to stay, the bits accumulate, the cat returns . . . I live in hope.

THE BANK

Now that my mother is ninety-four with Death lapping at her ankles, she is naturally getting into a bit of a flap over money and wills. She wants to know what has happened to her life's savings and how they're getting along, and she thinks, foolish innocent, that she can ring her local bank and someone will tell her.

Oh, ha ha! For starters the local branch doesn't even have its own phone number, only a central number. We phone, we wait, we press buttons, we get through, but all for nothing. They haven't the foggiest about investments. We must phone elsewhere – one number for ISAs, another for Tessas, another for these bonds, another for those bonds, until at last, exhausted and maddened by the phoning maze, my mother finds, tragically, that her savings are dwindling like a snowflake in a blast furnace.

How has this come about? When she moved here from Hove, her savings had to move with her, so we took advice, silly us, from the bank. But over the years, my mother has suspected that things were not going according to plan. So we wrote and told them what we wanted, but nothing happened. Why? Because they never received our letter, they swear it. And deterred by the telephone nightmare, the monster queues in the bank and the vicious, swarming traffic wardens who patrol around it, I have neglected to take my mother along there to investigate.

At last we are on their case. 'Why has my mother's investment shrunk rather than grown over the years?' we ask. 'Because you haven't left it in long enough,' answers the bank cheerily. Now the letters ISA are poison to us, we are in a molten fury and have arranged a meeting with a bevy of bank staff. Then we can give them a drubbing, tell them where to stick their ISAs, take out my mother's remaining pence, hide them under the mattress and never go near a bank again.

Meanwhile letters have been flooding in thanking my mother for opening more bonds. What bonds? She hasn't moved from her room or signed anything for weeks, and what could she buy bonds with anyway, now that the bank has left her with flumpence?

'Money makes money,' my father used to say. Not if you put it in this bank, it doesn't.

VIAGRA FOR GIRLS

Rosemary has been reading about Viagra for women. She was horrified. She could hardly bear to contemplate the paragraph on swollen
bits and blood. 'Where is the magic?' she asked later in a heart-rending way, shuddering at the word 'engorged'. Anyway, Rosemary had
assumed that the menopause came along to save us from all that. So
had Olga. It has been her salvation. Since the darling menopause she
has lost the annoying desire to go to bed with unsuitable men. She
was drawn to them like iron filings to a magnet and it brought her no
happiness. So neither she nor Rosemary were expecting any more
'magic' of that kind, but nowadays the pressure is on to keep trying.
Lots of people do. My mother has seen them on telly.

'It's that man with the pump again!' she shouts from her bedroom. 'He's on all these programmes.' Rosemary and I still prefer
singing. We have a bit of a problem talking about bodily functions in
a forthright way, let alone getting them to work. So naturally
Rosemary was thrilled to hear from her friend Elsie in Reading, who
had just been to hear a university dean extolling the beauty of the
flaccid penis. Rosemary and I had a scream in the kitchen. We have
more problems here. We are not sure about the beauty of the penis,
flaccid or otherwise.

Apparently the dean had been lecturing on the place of the
human body in religion. He was relaying a new idea, big in America
at present, that a fellow should learn to feel equally male in the above
condition and grow to appreciate his passive and gentle side. He recommended two helpful American books.

Wonderful. Another New Thought from the New World. Where
would we be without America? And hopefully the last thing a passive
and gentle fellow wants is some woman thundering in mad with

lust, so no Viagra for them or their wives. Lucky them. Meanwhile my friend Fielding hardly dares go out to the shops in case some Viagra-crazed woman, front bottom aflame, pounces on him from across the road. And even if she finds someone more appreciative, what about those side effects: splitting headaches, blue vision, red face, bulging eyes, swollen necks, damaged retinas, blackouts and death?

We need that dean, touring England, lecturing away and advocating 'flaccid'. Quickly, please!

TWIRLERS

Last week I found my mother lying in bed blubbing in the middle of the day. 'I'm depressed,' she cried poignantly. 'All my friends are dead!' So I ordered her to get up and make a steamed jam pudding, which she did in a trice and it snapped her out of the doldrums. Cooking is a lifesaver to my mother. When she was nearly dead with pneumonia, she spotted Ken Hom cooking prawns on telly, sat up at once and demanded a Chinese takeaway. So even I have dredged up a bit of enthusiasm. I have this new fad of various warm bits on salad. I tried to tell Rosemary about it on our dog walk but she was horrified. 'No!' she shouted. 'Not *recipes*! It's almost as bad as *routes*!'

Her daughter, who has moved to the East End, likes to chat forever about routes from there to here. Usually it is men who like to discuss routes, because they tend to know a better route than you do and will even argue with signposts. 'No, I wouldn't go that way. Always avoid the M11 and that Stansted turn-off. You should take the A10 to Ipswich and blah blah . . .

I often have vicious rows with Gardener about routes. He likes to go twirling about the back streets avoiding this, that and the other, whereas I like to zoom straight down the High Street and get home in a flash. But a Twirler cannot take a direct route, even at 1 a.m. when the roads are completely deserted. He must widdle all around the houses and back streets, via the Hebrides, until the passenger, who knows a much better, quicker way, is busting with silent rage or screaming and nutting the passenger window and could have walked home in half the time. I bet scores of relationships have foundered on a long, twirly journey. Or on a recipe.

I notice that a Twirler cannot even go straight through a recipe, but must add his own extras. Yesterday I was slaving away in the kitchen, sticking to the blessed Delia's every instruction, when Gardener drifted in suggesting alternatives and hurled extra bits of his own into my stew, without permission. Luckily he has, so far, never redirected one of my mother's recipes. That would be a direct route to the end of the road.

BIG NOISE

Last week I took my mother to the cinema for a treat. She never wishes to go again. The noise almost dashed her brains to pieces, and she is not a stranger to loud noise. For a start she is a shouter. A lifetime of shouting and roaring has taken its toll and left her with only one vocal chord. And here in Temper Towers, shouting, barking, blaring televisions and door-slammings are the norm. But the cinema adverts and *Gladiator* trailer were too much for her. Adverts, for some odd reason, are ten times louder than film volume, which is at eardrum-killer pitch anyway. And this was one of the quieter cinemas.

The trouble is that half the world is now partially deaf. The younger half. To them a squillion decibels, pain and tinnitus means pleasure. So what bad luck for Rosemary that she has a young pop-star girly living over her head with a loud voice, a barking dog, a DJ boyfriend and a penchant for staggeringly loud music played mainly at night.

Rosemary is in hell. Just as she was settling into her new home, the blasting noise ruined everything. Even complaining is a battle. One cannot gain access. The pop-star girly can't hear her bell ringing or the battering on her door, because her big television, hi-fi or mixers are on non-stop at earthquake volume. Eventually Rosemary and the young fellow from the top floor got together to tell her off. They dashed along and rapped at the pop-starlette's door in a brief gap in the tumult, but only the DJ boyfriend was in, playing loudly with his mixers.

'Bit loud last night. Sorry, mate,' said the upstairs boy and gave the DJ boyfriend an understanding wink. When one is a hip young fellow, there is no point siding with an old bat with a posh voice, even

145

if you promised to and her health and sanity depend on it.

I have tried to boss Rosemary into more aggressive action: thunderous retaliatory noise, a crowd of heavies, me and my mother, the council noise patrol, or even a leak to the tabloids, but she is too weedy. So the next day she slipped a polite note under the door begging for quiet. Fat chance. Apparently, noise is the new silence, says Fielding. 'Only a background hum, of course.' Oh, well. That's all right then.

FEET – THE SEQUEL

The other day I found my mother in a grim mood. She was peering at an ancient diary. 'This is the crematorium number,' she said, poking fiercely at the page. 'You'll need to know it soon. How are you going to find it?'

While I was out on my dog walk, she had woken in a panic and phoned Rosemary. 'What's Michele got to do first?' she croaked. 'Phone the crematorium or phone the rabbi?' 'Undertaker first,' snapped Rosemary, but then what? Rosemary didn't know. She has only ever had to deal with churches and vicars in a leisurely way, but if you are Jewish things have to be organised at a cracking pace. We will have only two days to get the show on the road, so it is vital to have an efficient plan of action.

It was my mother's feet making her desperate. They had throbbed and stabbed all night and by morning they looked like red and purple sausages. None of her shoes fit any more, she is forced to slob around in raggedy old sandals and will have to totter to her bridge game, planned for the weekend, looking like a tramp. And it's been boiling hot and she hasn't been able to face the shoe shop. No wonder she is losing the will to live.

But for once we were in luck. While out shopping I found the absolute perfect sandals for my mother: Velcro everywhere, in the favourite colours, navy and turquoise, with lovely soft soles. I rushed home with them, they fitted perfectly, the sausage feet had shrunk considerably and my mother shall go to bridge looking chic. The crematorium diary has been put away. Another reprieve.

But in this house it is one fright after another. My mother threatens to leave this earth, then the Daughter threatens to leave the country. She has nearly finished her studies and is planning another gap year. I had always believed that a parent need only endure one gap year, but now I must sweat through another – imagining my child on long-haul flights to distant war zones, repressive regimes, malarial swamps, pestered by sharks, jellyfish, muggers, kidnappers or dope smugglers, or pale and weeping behind bars in the Bangkok Hilton.

I bet I've inherited this sort of anxiety from my mother. Hopefully, I haven't inherited her feet.

HAPPY BIRTHDAY

When Olivia was young, she thought fifty was horribly old and that sixty was nearly dead. Now that she is nearly fifty, the goalposts seemed to have moved: eighty seems fairly old and ninety seems nearly dead. But my mother was ninety-five last week and her life is still a thrill a minute.

We didn't think it was going to be. We just tottered out for the usual birthday Chinese dinner in the favourite restaurant where we've already had three Last Birthdays and where the proprietor knows us by heart, ordered the usual prawns, my mother's hernia played up in the usual way, making her gulp and hiccup and almost faint at table. Cousin from the north thought the Reaper had arrived, a hush fell upon the restaurant, but then my mother recovered and the waitress approached with a special birthday surprise, covered by a silver lid.

What could it be? Waitress whisked off the lid and there it was. A Penis Birthday Cake, made from a large banana fritter and two apple fritters, sprinkled with a little crispy seaweed. We all had a scream. When one is ninety-five it is not usual to have a Penis Birthday Cake, but my mother was thrilled. She merrily blew out her candle and sliced off some banana.

I must here commend Daughter's boyfriend, who was the only chap at table and did not flinch. But I noticed some pallid and grumpy-looking diners at the table next to us. They were trying to have a quiet romantic dinner, with us screaming coarsely at the penis cake.

So there are all sorts of bizarre pleasure that Olivia can still look forward to. There is always an electric buggy, if you fancy life in the fast lane. Not knowing that the Chinese outing would be so wild, I borrowed a buggy to whizz my mother across the Heath. She was hugely ungrateful.

'You're stopping me walking!' she shouted grumpily. 'I've got to keep walking.' So we had a little squabble, drove to the Heath, commandeered the buggy and my mother zoomed off, almost crashing into the dog and running over the Daughter's ankle. And she had thought she would never drive again. At ninety-five, the possibilities are endless. So perhaps ninety-seven is very old and a hundred and ten is nearly dead. Olivia is only halfway.

DIETERS

One snag about the summer – it brings out the dieters. We take off our clothes, look at our pallid, flabby limbs and start dieting. But it's not just about fat. It's a sort of late spring clear-out of the innards. Now that the sky is blue and the sun shining, no one wants to be plugged up with rubbish. So Olivia is planning a cabbage-soup diet, Olga is on a crushed-pineapple-only diet, my mother is on a get-rid-of-arthritis diet, I am being vegetarian and my friend Clayden is on a blood-group-A diet, which means no meat, wheat or dairy produce, because he is descended from agricultural Neolithic tribes.

This is all terrifically time-consuming. First of all you must read the books, study the theory, then trail around searching for bizarre grains, pretend tea, soya this and that, then spend the rest of your life in the kitchen diddling about with ninety different recipes, to suit everybody's fancy.

Sometimes people may overreact in a house of dieters and go out of their way to eat rubbish. This is exactly what Fielding has done. He deliberately overdoses on carcinogenic salami, crisps and other filth and is now so toxic that anything healthy tastes repellent to him and he would rather die than enter the health-food shop, where women wear knitted skirts and no one can spell 'recieve' correctly.

Perhaps he is on the right track. I am finding this dieting something of a pain in the bum. I can't just slap on a quick chop any more, because my mother may not have red meat, wheat, caffeine, sugar, alcohol, citrus fruits, dairy products or even potatoes. I live mainly on wheat, caffeine, alcohol, dairy products and potatoes. Daughter cannot live without roast dinners and puddings and at the word 'tofu' she runs screaming from the house.

Fortunately it seems that after an initial spurt, these diets tend to fade out, rather like government initiatives. My mother has already rejected her gluten-free muesli, Clayden is guzzling toast for breakfast, Olga never wants to see another pineapple and Olivia has repeatedly postponed her no-alcohol cabbage diet, because it makes you faint, gives you dreadful wind and she cannot fit it in between parties.

DECORATING

Daughter is home from university. In her little room on campus, she was able to maintain a high standard of cleanliness, tidiness and good taste. But while she has been away, standards here have fallen. The halls and stairs are cluttered, there are dog toys scattered about the floors, the tasteless melange of furniture is covered with dreary throws covered in dog hairs or made into nests by the dog and Gardener, moths flit about and dust mites clog the elderly carpets.

These horrors unite Daughter and my mother. They both feel isolated here, ashamed to invite their friends home to tea. My mother can only play away bridge matches and Daughter must quickly whisk her friends upstairs, through the slum quarters to her haven of taste and cleanliness on the top floor.

She cannot live like this. It is insupportable. Our home must be decorated. At once. She cannot understand the delay. She's been begging for decoration since Christmas, but she doesn't understand how the world works.

Before we could paint the hall, the flat roof needed to be done, and to do that we needed the ashphalters, who were all busy, because now the summer is here and the rain over, everybody wants their roof done, so we were in a queue for the ashphalters, but at last they arrived – at dawn on my mother's birthday. Now we have to wait for the builders and decorators, who are trailing round after the asphalters.

I don't mind. My wallet has been haemorrhaging money and I'm quite keen to have a breather before the next ghastly bout of decorating – which means more shopping, choosing paint colours, rows about the colours, then the new carpet, more colour choosing and rowing, then hammerings, drilling, clatterings, people clumping up and down stairs for days on end, and more terrifying expenditure.

But Daughter cannot be held in check. If the decorators can't come, then she'll decorate herself. She is in there like the Light Brigade. She is like her grandma, a human tornado. This quality has skipped a generation. It has missed me out. I like to nestle quietly in my little slum, while the house decays peacefully around me, but those two like to roar about, bossing, shouting and improving things.

INSURANCE FRAUD

I am fifty-nine and drive a car worth two shillings around locally to transport my elderly mother or the shopping. I need to reinsure my car, third-party only, advises the garage, because it's such a croc. Foolishly, I put 'writer' as my job description.

Insurance company takes my money and then asks exactly what sort of writer I am. I tell them. My premium shoots up sixty per cent! It is now more expensive than comprehensive was. Obviously some mistake.

I ring and describe my lifestyle: I stay indoors and write about old age and girls. Last week I attended a 105th birthday party. Sometimes, when I'm feeling really wild, I go and collect an Indian takeaway and drink half a pint of shandy. I do not visit war zones, riots or protests, I never investigate crime. I never enter pubs, rarely drink, never take drugs and never exceed the speed limit. I haven't made a claim for twenty-five years. Now will they please reduce my premium?

No. I am still a writer and any writer is a huge risk. So is anyone in the theatre, or in TV, radio or films. Disappointingly my friend Sylvia agrees. 'Writers drink,' says she. They pile into bars and pubs in Fleet Street, their ties askew, noses red, and then they stagger out and crash their cars. I remind Sylvia that the Fleet Street she knew has long gone. I am being unfairly penalised.

I ask which profession is not risky? This seems to be a bit of a mystery. Insurance lady doesn't know for sure. (Neither does the Ombudsman, the Society of Insurers or the AA.) They all sound rather cagey, but someone at lasts lets slip that teachers are not high risk. Nor are civil servants.

Fielding is outraged. I stay at home with my mummy, he goes daily into the hell of a London comprehensive, and my lifestyle is considered more dangerous than his. What rubbish. I refuse to pay sixty per cent extra. I change my insurers. Easier said than done. There's a catch. I must still pay a huge escape fee to the original robber insurers for insuring me for one fortnight at the inflated amount that I had never agreed to. Now where is my old bicycle?

HOT FAMILY LIFE

Yesterday morning on our dog walk I was moaning on at Sylvia about the state of play in our house. It is life on the San Andreas fault. One never knows when the tectonic plates are going to grate and clash. When the weather is baking hot and one has several tricky personalities crammed into one house, there are countless clash possibilities.

My mother, Daughter and I like to pile things in the sink, Gardener likes to stack them neatly on the draining board; the dog and Gardener like to slump on the sofa and crush the cushions, my mother demands neatly plumped cushions; Daughter wants the house decorated at once, I don't give a monkey's when it's decorated and my mother has given up all hope of gracious living.

Everyone thinks everyone else should be doing things that they haven't done yet, but we can't do what everyone else wants, because we each have our own priorities, which nobody else understands.

Under these conditions, it is difficult to have a relaxed meal. Daughter is seething, Gardener is stony-faced, I am waiting for the clash, my mother is simmering upstairs, the dog is begging and crying for snacks and, more often than not, I am missing *EastEnders*.

Olivia is also having a tough time domestically. Yesterday she came sweating home from the shops feeling fat, only to find her kitchen full of grown-up children, cooking. Once upon a time this was her domain – empty, clean and quiet. Now it's all fry-ups and *Naked Chef*. The place reeks of coconut milk, lemon grass and chillies. She is an outsider in her own kitchen.

'That's family life,' says Sylvia breezily. 'You'll all miss it when it's gone.' Sylvia lives with one properly adult daughter, on a separate floor, and usually just the cat and dog. It sounds like heaven. But she may be right. Rosemary has just spent four months alone in her new flat without a child or elderly relative to look after. She lived a sort of desolate half life, dragging herself to work and back. Luckily the son has now come home.

'I love ironing his T-shirt,' whispers Rosemary rather ashamed and going pink, 'and taking his phone messages. Don't you think I look better?' Oh, dear.

HOLIDAY PLANS

In a few weeks Gardener and I are going on holiday. We have never done this before. It has thrown my mother into a panic. Not only will I be up in a perilous aeroplane, but Daughter will be left in charge of the house and dog and my mother will be boarded out.

The potential for tragedy is immense: my plane may crash, Daughter will leave the doors unlocked and the lights/gas/candles on all night; robbers will pour in, the house will burn down/blow up, and my mother herself will become terminally ill/die while I'm away. She can almost feel the illness welling up already. It could even strike just as I set off for the airport, my holiday will be cancelled and my mother will never forgive herself for ruining things.

Actually, she quite fancies a break. The building and decorating work, state of disrepair and screeching at our house have been getting her down and we have found a divine rest home nearby with charming ground-floor room available, French windows leading out into a heavenly rose garden and lawns. There's a doctor round the corner, some of her chums are already there, she needn't even miss bridge and all this is at bargain price. But it's no good. She's already gone into anxiety overdrive. On permanent hyper-alert, she can spot a calamity coming, and Gardener has almost caused one already.

Yesterday he dragged a large and mouldering folding table into the hall. He had spotted it in a skip and fell in love with it at once. But it caused uproar at our house.

'It'll have woodworm!' cried my mother, grabbing for the angina spray, 'and if it's in his room, they'll crawl out and eat straight through the floor boards and it'll fall through the floor and land on your harpsichord!'

She would bet her life on it, and just our luck that I'll be tinkling away at the keyboard when it crashes through, I'll be killed and it'll all be Gardener's fault. His copybook is soaked with blots. And worse still, he gets to go on holiday, the dog stays at home to be pampered by Daughter and my poor mother is sent off to boarding kennels. She has always thought that life was neither right nor fair. Now she has been proved correct.

BOWEL TROUBLE

The dog has joined my mother in her anti-holiday protest. It is probably a subconscious protest. They both have violent bowel disorders. My mother has spent the greater part of the week on the lavatory and the dog has just done something so frightful on its walkie that I had to rush it straight to the vet. So my holiday is dangling in the balance. How can I go away and leave them in such a state?

I am beginning to feel rather bogged down by it all. There is nothing like a bit of body malfunction to lower the spirits, and in our house, bowels seem to be the big problem. Somebody or other is always bound to have something going wrong in that area, which needs medicine or special dietary requirements and discussion – including description and moaning. The cupboard is stuffed with Fybogel, Dioralyte, Preparation H, Beano, Gaviscon and such like, to cope with any eventuality.

Once, when I was going nearly mad, I visited a psychotherapist. 'Your mother's currency is shit,' said she strictly. She may have been right. In our house, lavatories have always been high on the agenda. A bidet has always been a must. In Ruislip in the early fifties we were pioneers. We had the first bidet. Visitors assumed it to be an odd sort of lavatory or foot bath.

I now know that in other homes, this problem area is rarely up for discussion. Any other bodily discomfort may be referred to, but not this sort. I mention the current state of play in our bowels and other people are sickened. Fielding and Rosemary shudder and beg me to shut up and Fielding says that in his house, psychologically, there is no lavatory.

At least we are in good company. Dr Johnson had terrible bowel problems. He recorded everything he imbibed or expelled, liquid or solid, in his diary — in Latin. *Hodie multum durum est*, he often wrote. Poor thing. It was his morphine turning everything to concrete. What a life he must have had. My mother is sick of her life. She sees the spectre of incontinence looming and wants to die, preferably tonight and not in a pool of excrement. She is now too ill to go to the heavenly bargain respite home, and must go instead to the squillion-pound-a-week nursing home. Such is the mood in our house as my holiday approaches. Will we make it?

THE RETURN

Back from hols. What a shock it is — the dreary chores, the stinking traffic and the grisly news on telly. Only days ago I was floating in a quiet blue pool in the sunny hills of Greece, or picking grapes and pomegranates. But my mother is thrilled that I'm back. It means the end of her stay in kennels.

It was the same old story — charming but overworked, ever-changing staff, severely incapacitated residents unable to chat, horrid stewed tea, and worst of all — last meal of the day at five-thirty, usually white-bread ham sandwiches. This is not the meal of choice for an elderly Jewish person with delicate innards. Naturally my mother complained fiercely and demanded alternatives. She became pack leader of the malcontents, and why not? Her stay cost half the Royal Mint. For that she deserved more than measly sandwiches. Someone was coining it, and it wasn't the staff.

We had looked at another residence, cheaper but far worse — with that horrible thick smell of wee that sticks in your nose, residents shambling about, hair in greasy strands, dreary wrong-size clothes, mumbling to themselves. And a grubby, cell-like room for my mother. So we whisked her to the palace instead.

'Are you self-financing?' asked the manageress. Yes. But obviously not for long. A couple of months here and my mother would be a pauper. Then she'd presumably be thrown out to live in wee-wee land and sit in a brown armchair. I realise I would rather she stayed at home — even if doubly incontinent and nearly dead.

So it was with some relief that she greeted my return. So did the Daughter. She and Boyfriend had looked after the dog during my absence, had a small party, cleansed the house from top to bottom and were soon completely fagged out.

'Tell your mum it was a breeze,' advised Boyfriend, but Daughter couldn't. She, like her mother and grandmother, likes to tell all. 'It was the worst two weeks of my life,' said she dramatically. 'I don't know how you do it!' Good. This is what I like to hear.

But my mother is soon back in the dumps. Knackered by her struggle for justice in the kennels, she retires to bed. 'This tea tastes bitter,' she moans weedily. 'Those flowers clash.' How quickly things return to normal.

STROKE

My mother is in hospital again. We spend more and more time there as the years go by. But there is one development we're not too keen on: mixed wards. How horrid, when one is trying to use a commode, protected from public view by only a thin, wibbly curtain, to know that there are strange men in pyjamas only feet away. And just diagonally across the ward is the occasional array of male genitalia. My mother is desperate to have her curtain drawn to shield her from it. The risk of a glimpse of gaping pyjamas, or bits and pieces with tubes attached, is a terrible worry for women brought up in more modest times.

Also, a rather suspect fellow in baseball cap and nightie comes lurching along regularly, his leg in a grubby plaster-cast, wanting to chat. Elderly ladies blanch and tremble as he draws near. And an inebriate male often stumbles past, grovelling suspiciously in his trousers. Neither of these fellows is helping my mother on the road to recovery.

Otherwise, this ward is much as usual: kind and overworked nurses, droves of patients, in a hospital run on the Third World model, with relatives providing various necessities: pillow cases, extra pillows, vases, nappies. Daughter was rather shocked on her first visit. 'We're taking her home,' said she strictly, going a bit white around the gills. 'She can't stay here.' But she must. She's had a stroke, is attached to a drip and cannot speak.

This is a terrible impediment for my mother. Not only is chatting her favourite pastime, but next morning she has a gripping instalment to tell and can't. Nearby patients fill me in. They have all had the night from hell, with one wandering lady wrenching everyone's bedclothes off, tripping over her own knickers, crashing to the floor, blood everywhere. Meanwhile, up at the other end of the ward, the inebriate smuggled in cans of lager, drank heavily and attacked the nurse with a poker. Naturally, my mother and surrounding ladies were grey-faced and weeping with exhaustion.

But the poor nurses, doctors and patients battle on bravely, rather like a community in war time: ill-equipped, managed by incompetents and at the mercy of maniacs. 'It's just the real world,' says my friend Alison. No wonder my mother wants to hide under the bedclothes.

STROKE GLOOM

No wonder my mother was in a glum mood last week. Since her stroke she had been spoon fed slop in what she presumed to be the antechamber to Death. The puréed hospital dinners were getting her down and she had been signalling fiercely that they be thrown out of the window.

But now things are looking up. She has been moved to a ladies-only ward and has fallen in love with the speech therapist. The horrid food tube up her nose is to come out, the puréed slop has been replaced by squishy dinners. The hairdresser has called and my mother no longer looks like the wild witch of the woods.

Of course life is still not all fun. 'I feel like a baby,' burbles my mother as I spoon in some mush. 'I don't want to live like this!' But hey, let's be positive! Last week she couldn't even have spoken to me at all. And with any luck, life won't be like this for too long. Once she can swallow and eat, she can come home.

But first she must learn to eat slowly, small mouthfuls, not talk with her mouth full and swallow properly. After ninety-five years of eating at top speed while yabbering non-stop, my mother finds this tricky. So we practise in hospital. 'Finish your mouthful!' I roar. 'Do not speak! Swallow twice!'

'Loody hell!' shouts my mother.

'Shut up!' yells the woman in the next bed.

'Fughy iddiloh!' shouts my mother. The ward is in uproar. But it all calms down. Everyone apologises. Chocolates and sedatives are passed round.

There was a time when I didn't know what a stroke was. In the the long list of my father's final illnesses, the strokes and heart attacks all seemed to blur in together. But now I know. A stroke is the one that can paralyse you down one side, make you talk rubbish, or stop speaking and dribble bits of food out of the side of your mouth. It kills more women than breast cancer and is the biggest cause of disability. Make mine a heart attack any day. Not far from my mother is another elderly stroke sufferer who cannot speak or eat at all. She must be fed through a tube directly into her stomach. So we are called the lucky ones.

HOUSE OF STRESS

I have had a headache for weeks on end. At 3 a.m. if you have a roasting, splitting headache, it is difficult not to think 'tumour' or 'brain haemorrhage'. It's only a stiff neck, said the doctor. 'Go and have a massage.' I had one, my headache vanished and I told Rosemary the good news, but she was horrified. She backed away as if from a maniac.

'Your headache has gone because your mother got out of hospital this morning,' she snapped strictly. 'You refuse to think psychogenically!'

These alternative remedies are beginning to get Rosemary down. Here I am having massages and feelings for trees, her daughter has just returned clapping and chanting from Dance Camp Wales and her other daughter chants and dances for a living *and* meditates. But Rosemary finds massage particularly sickening. If there's anything she loathes it's having someone wrenching and pummelling at her body, drizzling oils and aromas and playing soothing tinkly music.

Until now I have agreed with her, but the massage worked for a while, and anyway Rosemary was wrong. The headache soon came roaring back, even though my mother was home again. So I tried an Indian head massage for myself *and* Daughter. Why not? We live in the House of Stress. My mother has a mystery galloping rash, Daughter has a puzzling recurrent sore throat and the dog has diarrhoea. It is difficult to cope with all this with a throbbing head and rigid neck full of knots.

The Indian massage worked absolute magic. Daughter and I floated out into the Holloway Road. I had a new face and neck, my headache disappeared properly and the atmosphere in our home for the rest of the day was heavenly. No squabbles, no weeping, shouting or crabby remarks, the dog's bowels were soon in order and my mother's rash subsided.

If only Rosemary could endure a head massage. Now her Auntie has fallen downstairs carrying all the family porcelain, Rosemary is having some problems and her mood and posture are very poor. We both tend to stoop and have a poking tortoise neck and if we don't watch out we shall soon have widows' humps. But talk of yoga or Alexander technique throws Rosemary into a bate. She stamps off and grabs for her cigarettes. Of course there is an acupuncture point for smoking. I wonder . . .

SPEECHLESS

My mother is home from hospital at last, so I take her to visit her old friends, who have just moved to London from the south coast. They think north London a dismal place and wept for three days when they arrived. Outside their window they can see the filthy roaring traffic instead of the heavenly quiet streets of Hove. My mother also longs to moan about stinky London, but bad luck, it's only a few weeks since her stroke and she still can't chat. So she clings to her friend, kissing, blubbing and garbling.

What an emotional reunion! My mother hasn't seen these chums for years. Now her friend can hardly walk and my mother can hardly speak. But oddly enough, she is not suicidal. Perhaps because she has at last found some chums who are still alive and can move about. And with a bit of miming, signing, burbling, croaking and me translating, she can just about converse. So things are looking up. And at least my mother can shout expletives with bell-like clarity. What luck that her brain manages to dredge up 'bollocks' every time she needs it. This is tremendously useful when all the other words get lost in the mist.

Isn't the brain fascinating? We are learning all about it. Apparently it stores words in groups, so when my mother needs *fork*, up comes *knife* instead. She needs *him*, she gets *her*. But *bollocks* is always retrievable and so is *bloody hell*. These words are lifesavers when one cannot answer the phone, make a simple request, read a book or write a note, and yesterday my mother needed them desperately, while trying to demonstrate the cooking of fish-cakes. She has tried to do this for years but I have never quite got the hang of it. Now she must do it without a voice.

What hell in the kitchen. My mother drew small circles in the air, made wild V-signs and stirring motions, while Gardener and I looked blank. 'Small!' she shouted. 'Round!' More blank looks. She tore at her hair and roared, 'Bollocks!' And then we got it. Two eggs! Correct. My mother was in heaven. But we are stuck in an endless game of charades. We are now experts. Will we still be playing it twenty-four hours a day next Christmas? We bloody hope not.

TREBUS MEMORIAL LIBRARY

Last year a striking gentleman called Mr Trebus appeared on telly. He lived in a house stuffed with treasured items which the rest of the world called stinking rubbish. I notice that Gardener's room is very similar, but without the stink. So far.

Gardener has always collected strange items: twigs, stones, scraps of paper, rag and crumpled tin. He deposits them in little clumps and calls them 'arrangements'. It is dangerous to send Gardener to the tip with rubbish, because he tends to return laden with new debris for his 'arrangements'. Now he's taken to collecting dead flowers. He darts about looking anxious, checking vases and begging us not to throw mouldering flowers away.

Inside Gardener's room, excess arrangement material crunches underfoot and the desk is densely cluttered with arrangements. Oddly enough he is proud of his room and calls it the Trebus Memorial Library.

Naturally this creates tension in our home. For a start, Daughter must pass by this room with friends on her way upstairs, and should the door be open, everyone will see inside and know that we're harbouring a strange creature and our house is weird, when Daughter so longs for us to appear normal.

And of course it distresses my mother. She sees mounds of rubble going in, but nothing coming out, so where is it all going? One day, Gardener's room will explode, spraying debris all over the hall and garden. Yesterday she spotted him dragging the wreckage of a chair into the basement while I was out. She reported him the minute I returned. She suspects that the Trebus Library contents are spreading like a Quatermass into the rest of the house. Soon health and safety persons will be round in their white overalls, to order a clear-out and expose us on telly.

'We'd never have guessed!' neighbours will say. 'He kept himself to himself. They seemed pleasant enough.' My mother and Daughter will be unable to bear the shame.

Meanwhile, our home is simmering with repressed hatreds. Or ringing with expressed hatreds, but Gardener's arrangements are only intensifying with age, so it's either divorce for me, or arrangements for everyone. In Gardener's childhood, he and his siblings played in a large shed. He has tried, ever since, to create a feeling of shed wherever he lives. The usual place for a shed is in the garden. Perhaps . . .

OUR HOSPITAL

What a surprise to see our very own local hospital on telly last week. My mother pointed excitedly at the screen. There was the A&E entrance that we know so well. We're all in and out of the place like yo-yos: my mother with her angina, broken back and stroke, Rosemary with her broken ankle, Olivia with a fish bone stuck in her throat, me for this and that test, and we're all still alive.

In fact we're rather fond of the place. Half our street works there – doctors, nurses, even a moral philosopher. I bumped into a neighbour/nurse the other day. 'Do you want to know the truth?' she asked. You bet. She told me some riveting details. 'And it's all documented.' Poor hospital. It has been much maligned, because although we've had the odd wretched experience in there – the long wait in casualty or for a bedpan, the horrid puréed dinners, we've all been looked after, cured and called back for check-ups and therapies.

I haven't even spotted any ageism. At ninety-five my mother often longs to be allowed to fade away, but our hospital seems to pull out all the stops to keep her going. So this is a little hymn of praise to the Whittington Hospital. And to the NHS. In the last few months we have been a tremendous drain on its resources: my mother's stroke, Daughter's mystery lump, me with eye problems. GPs have been buzzing round here for red alerts – the vomiting virus, the after-stroke frights, the chemist has been churning out pills, and all of it free, except for a couple of prescriptions. Of course the food's probably better in France but we're not moaning.

So I'm a little ashamed of the tantrums I've sometimes had in our divine hospital. Rosemary has been disgusted at my lack of forbearance. I once left my mother mouldering in a queue in outpatients and rang Rosemary sobbing from the foyer. 'I can't stand it any

175

more. I'm sick of f . . . ing hospitals!'

'Pull yourself together,' snapped Rosemary, and rushed to join me for a cigarette and a shout on the hospital lawn. She herself never behaves badly, however long the queue. She just gazes admiringly at the nurses, remembering their rotten wages and dedication. I shall now try to follow her example.

SWIMMING

My mother was moaning poignantly at the doctor the other day. She can't ride horses or motorbikes any more, she can't drive, dance, play bridge, walk about, cook or talk. We both wept in unison. Doctor got out the tissues and explained. When one is ninety-five, there are a few hobbies that one has to give up on. But there is one possibility left. Swimming. Anyone can float about. And we have a leisure pool with beach-type access just up the road.

This is the plus side of being ninety-five. What better time to take risks and try extreme sports? So I take my mother to the pool. In normal life, this is my leisure activity from hell: the crowds, the shrieking, the belting pop music, the echo, puddles, swamp atmosphere and swirling germs, soggy towels and clothes, the struggle with the lockers. I've done it all before when the Daughter was little. Now here we are again.

I shove my mother into the madhouse changing rooms. Will she crack up and scream to go home, like I used to do? No. She is calm and relaxed. She changes and we tunnel our way through the scrum into the pool and heaven. The water is almost empty, the sodden, screeching public have left. That was them in the changing rooms.

'Cripples' hour,' says my mother cheerily, gazing at the turquoise water. She glides in on a special amphibious wheelchair. Paradise. This morning she looked like a corpse, now she looks like Esther Williams. But as she glides along, a large beachball lands inches from her head. She roars at the hooligans responsible. They put their ball away at once and swim for cover. What a miracle. The voiceless cripple can now move and shout.

Perhaps Fielding should join us next time. He's been having a rather traumatic time in his ordinary swimming pool. A large show-off in the next lane kept overtaking and kicking Fielding as he passed. How enraging, when one is trying to relax, to be repeatedly kicked by someone so large and muscular that one dare not tell them off.

I suspect that my mother would have done. Not only is she emboldened by the miraculous swimming, but no one would have the nerve to publicly kick one of the oldest swimmers on earth. Even the Grim Reaper seems to have backed off. For now.

BANK TROUBLE

We are having more problems with the bank. We ring to ask about my mother's money, but they won't tell me a thing unless she answers some secret identification questions first. Naturally they suspect that I have her tied to the commode and am trying to swindle her out of her savings. So my mother tries to answer.

'What is your date of birth?'

'Gurble burble ten hundred and three, five, SIX!' she shouts triumphantly.

'June 10th!' I hiss into her ear. But the bank lady hears me.

'You're telling her,' says she strictly. 'I'm afraid I can't accept that.' Anyway, she has more questions to ask, but there's another snag. She's lost the questions. 'There's no information coming up on our computer,' says the bank lady. So even if my mother could answer clear as crystal, without me standing over her with a bull-whip, it would get us nowhere, because the bank has nothing to ask her. She is a non-person.

How difficult it is not to lose one's temper. Especially as the bank has pulled another fast one. They've cunningly sold my mother a bond, when she was ninety-four, that cannot be retrieved for several years. What were they thinking of? Now, should my mother need to squander her money on a thieving nursing home or give it to us instead, she won't be able to, because she can't get at a penny of it.

Why did we fall for such a silly trick? Because the bank adviser advised us to. Now the bank won't answer any questions unless I produce enduring power of attorney, or my mother, and visit them. Then they'll tell us everything – if it's on their computer. Has the dregs of my mother's money disappeared? Has my whole mother disappeared?

So we go. But it's too dangerous for us. The queue is so gigantic that my mother may die waiting or we'll get a parking ticket. Luckily there are advantages to being tremendously old. My mother looks weedy and starts to slump sideways. (I have trained her to do this. People then tend to take fright and attend to us more quickly.) Terrified bank staff promise that the manager will ring us at home.

Surprise, surprise! He does so, within the hour! My mother shall have her money back. Could this be a happy ending? From a bank? Watch this space.

SCREAMING

How difficult it is not to scream nowadays. The world is so annoying. Yesterday I had a very loud scream in the street, then came home and repeatedly banged my head against the armchair. How else is one to manage?

I had just taken my mother on another emergency dash to hospital because she awoke blind in one eye. One look at her date of birth and she was whizzed through A&E in a trice: nurses, doctors, tests, ultrasound — all in three hours, but then we had to go to the pharmacy, where a crowd of thousands waited for prescriptions. Outside the sun was shining, the dog waiting for walkies and lavatory, my work piling up, and there we were, stuck in the bowels of the hospital.

'Won't be long,' said the pharmacist, but what did that mean? Could be minutes, could be hours. It's *not knowing* that seems to bring on my breakdowns. So I stuck my poor, half-blind, wilting mother just inside the entrance and ran outside for a giant scream. In the roar of London's traffic, no one could really hear. Anyway, nowadays it is customary to ignore maniacs. People just walked by normally.

But I find that when I am screaming and going mad, it always helps if someone stops and sympathises. This has a magically calming effect. I know because it's happened before. I was once having a low, moaning scream while waiting for ever for a 49 bus. Terrified queuers clustered at the other end of the shelter, so I gave it a kicking, sat on the pavement and cried.

Along came a courageous elderly fellow and asked what the problem was. I told him, he sympathised. 'D'you know why this country's going down the pan?' said he. 'Because it's full of shit!' I cheered up at once. Then he asked me to go dancing, but I had to get to

Battersea.

Sadly, my mother had heard me screaming yesterday. 'I'm a bloody nuisance,' she croaked when we got home and wept with exhaustion. Fluorescent green slime from the hospital tests dribbled out of her eyes, rather like Hammer Horror. We had another desperate laugh, but one never knows what fun is in store. This morning a box of chocolates arrived, from the bank! How bizarre! Miracles can happen. Perhaps tomorrow my mother will be twenty-one again. She lives in hope.

INEFFECTUAL

Rosemary and I have discovered a sad fact: elderly ladies have no authority, especially over girls. Well, at least *we* haven't. Rosemary's tried polite and non-confrontational, I've tried screaming and offensive, but neither method works. The girls just do as they please.

Poor Rosemary. The minor celebrity girl living above her wakes at dawn, sleeps all afternoon, stays up all night, plays loud music, has a large barking dog and slams doors. Rosemary has hardly slept for months. She is almost demented. 'What shall I do?' she moans. 'I can't stand it!' She's tried to complain. Once.

'I don't give a shit about your life,' said the rude girl and leapt into a waiting taxi, leaving the upstairs music on.

Friends and neighbours have offered Rosemary advice: 'Give her a bollocking/wake the cow up in the afternoons/ring the council/tell the tabloids.' But Rosemary will do none of it. 'I've written her a note,' said she weedily. What is more enraging than a friend who begs for advice and then will not take it?

Meanwhile I am having an ongoing spat with rude girls in the park. They are ruining my dog walks. 'You've got dirty feet,' they called out last week. 'Erk. You're a crusty.' My mother was infuriated. She made angry roaring noises and waved her stick about but I stuffed her into the car. Modern rude girls do not give a fig for sick old ladies. I gave them a telling-off, but Rosemary disapproved.

'That was very provocative,' said she scornfully. 'You should have ignored them.' So I tried her advice. It was useless. Next day the rude girls were there again, sneering and making vile remarks. I ignored them, but the little stinkers formed a larger gang and water-bombed us.

I am not pleased. I've tried to be calm, liberal and grown-up, but my inner thug is busting to get out, rip their ears off and have them clamped into the stocks. Also I'm frightened, which makes me even crosser. How weedy to be frightened of girls. Perhaps Daughter can explain.

'They think you're an old lady. So they can beat you up. Not that you're old, Mum,' says she generously. 'You're just old to them.' Oh, thank you. 'I'll come with you for a dog walk,' says she fiercely. 'Nobody fucks with ME!' I bet they don't. She's a girl.

FOOTBALL GLOATERS

As our video cannot be trusted I raced home from a party just in time for my favourite programme. Why did I bother? The whole evening's programmes had been shoved aside by football, as usual. My mother was suicidal. Naturally I rang and complained, but I had to shout my complaint at an answerphone. 'I bet your blood pressure went up,' said Gardener, gloating.

This is another horrid thing about football enthusiasts. Other people's misery only intensifies their enjoyment. They adore a telly clogged with sports and hordes of bellowing, bullet-headed clots roaring in the pubs and streets. Anyone who doesn't is just an hysterical girly or spoil-sport.

I also detected scorn and gloating in the voice of the woman who rang back to answer my complaint. 'We haven't had many complaints this time,' said she rather snottily. 'In fact we have more complaints if we don't put the football on.'

This splurge of football is extra disappointing because I had just begun to feel cheery, thinking the demise of football was on the cards. ITV Digital has gone down the tubes and hopefully with it several football clubs. Rejoice. Serves them right for drowning players in money. I hear that in 1992 an admired think tank concluded that the British were 'essentially right wing or stupid'. When one watches the droves of football maniacs rampaging in their bobble hats, one cannot help but agree.

'There's nothing *you people* can do during the World Cup,' says Fielding, King of Gloaters. 'One piece of advice I've got for you. Get two tellies.' I already have two. 'Well, you're either part of mainstream culture, or you're living in a rarified and snobbish cul-de-sac,' says he laughing merrily. 'If you wish to converse with me, you better hurry, because I'll be off the radar until about June 2nd. But then we've got pre-season friendlies, the cricket season's looking promising, then there's Wimbledon, Beckham's foot's better . . . '

In the background I hear his wife and daughters screaming with rage and disgust. I had thought they liked football. 'They used to, but now the girls have grown up, they've got no interest at all,' says Fielding. The key words here are *grown up*. I smack the phone down. But Gardener snatches it up again. He desperately needs to drone at someone about last night's Italian football. Watch that soaring divorce rate.

FEAR OF FALLING

I'm just walking dowstairs in an ordinary way when suddenly, help! The foot slips, the body tumbles down and I'm left dangling by one arm from the bannister. What luck that I happened to be hanging on to it in the first place, so that I only had my arm practically wrenched from its socket, instead of a broken neck.

I stagger out to meet Sylvia for our dog walk. She is also tottering. Why? Because she also fell over this morning. For nothing. She was having her breakfast, got up for another cup of tea and fell over. Just like that! Sylvia's dog was distraught. It stood on her chest, kissing her and pinning her to the ground, when she was already severely bruised.

Meanwhile, Gardener is forever falling upstairs, Fielding falls over his cat and last week my mother's friend Cissy had just cleaned her kitchen, was standing admiring it, turned round to admire another sparkling surface, fell over and broke her arm. For no reason at all.

What is going on? I know really. In my youth I once fell off a huge and crotchety horse seven times in one hour without the tiniest bruising or breakage, but now, half a century later, we are all falling, even while stationary, our bones snapping like twigs and yards of flesh turning purple. Rosemary still has an aching red and purple foot from falling downstairs in 1997 with the ironing board.

'Why was she carrying an ironing board down the stairs?' snapped my mother crabbily. Because she was hurrying to watch Princess Diana's funeral.

My mother's crabbiness masked a fear of falling. This falling down business is making her a prisoner in her bedroom. Even with her stairlift, she dare not go downstairs and make herself tea if the house is empty. She would rather lie parched and starving in her room than go down those stairs, because odds on she'll fall over, break a limb and die in agony all alone. Then she has the nerve to fuss about me going out at night. But why worry about the two crack houses up by the station and the yobs and muggers crowding the streets, when one can almost die standing looking at one's own kitchen?

'And home is also where you get sexually abused and murdered,' says Rosemary breezily. Quick, let's all go out to play.

FILTHY WORLD

What a world! Fielding and I are close to despair. Poor Fielding was tapping away at his e-mail, expecting some pleasant messages, when up popped 'Amazing Anal – Tight Holes'. It gave him a bit of a turn. In his youth Fielding used to grow rather overheated looking at his mother's knitting-pattern book, so the modern welter of in-your-face sex/porn/filth on his monitor and telly makes him feel quite ill. 'You know – when you've just been sick and you go all cold and prickly. I tend to steer clear,' says he.

So do I. When I have the option. This morning I received 'Sexy Schoolgirls Getting Fucked', and Gardener got 'Holly Shit Porn for Only One Dollar'. He did not open it. It plainly contained abominations and probably a virus. Fielding and I are just scaredy-cat about the content. We have never been keen on even normal close-up body parts, but nowadays one cannot escape them. I was watching the news when on came a merry blonde weather girl. She wore a clinging pink top and had fairly large bosoms.

'It's a lovely day here,' said she pointlessly, 'and I'll be back in fifteen minutes with the weather.' What was she up to? It is later on that the channels are usually packed with bosoms. Sometimes I visit my mother's room late at night, she's fallen asleep, left the telly on and the screen is heaving with bodies doing heaven knows what. Daughter's girly magazines are crammed with blow-job instructions, her chum Dan finds odious porn hiding behind his browser, *The Sexual Life of Catherine M* is selling like hotcakes and this morning Fielding faced 'Do Me Doggie Style' and a backdrop of Kylie bottoms as he bought his milk and papers.

Now some fusspots have complained about prostitutes' cards in phone boxes. Why bother? The cards aren't all that obscene. I know because my dad used to collect them on his way home from the bookmaker. They weren't technicolour, they weren't live action, they were a modest size and they help your average sex-worker to stay safe indoors, rather than be out and about among the nutters. Anyway, no modern child would be seen dead in a phone box. They are all at home on their mobiles possibly staring at an unsolicited deluge of beastliness on screen. Please complain about *that*.

MADNESS

How easy it is to go barking mad nowadays. I nearly did it yesterday. First the computer plays up, then I have a flat tyre. What a sweat. Then into Gardener's car, which I can't drive properly. I'm late for my dog walk. The dog is off its head. Then back, then off to the fish shop, which is nearly closed. Only a few dull scraps of fish left, and on to my mother's stroke club. First visit for months.

I long to dump her there, come home and sit in a darkened cellar, but I can't. 'Don't leave me,' cries my mother pitifully. She is a baby on her first day at nursery school. But I can't hang about. I am a desperate woman and the fish is mouldering and stinking in the boiling car. I leave heartlessly, home to huge claps of thunder. Car alarms go off, the whole house shudders, the dog breaks down, and things haven't even hotted up yet.

I have bought Rosemary some fish. She comes to collect it – a few moments of pleasure as we admire my sunflowers and red-hot pokers at the sunny end of the garden. They have taken me years to cultivate and months of slug fighting to safeguard, but suddenly Rosemary strides towards them. She wants to try some blackberries beyond. In she goes, crashing through the undergrowth. Help! She is millimetres from my pokers!

'Get out! get out!' I scream rather crudely. 'You're like a bloody elephant!'

Rosemary is infuriated. 'I will not! How dare you!' She stands her ground, imperilling my prize sunflower. She grabs at a poker. Panic stations. More screaming. My mother also screams from her room. 'What the bloody hell's going on?' Meanwhile, upstairs Daughter is demonstrating her new hobby – whirling balls of flame about, splattering paraffin liberally across the wooden flat roof in front of an audience of chums, encouraged by loud pop music and Gardener. Now she too is enraged. Her screaming mother has ruined her show, alarmed the neighbours and embarrassed her friends. Shame.

What sort of a day is this? Rosemary blames me. I have no restraint. Why could I not just politely say 'Please mind my pokers'? I don't know. I blame the computer, flat tyre, flying fireballs, fish shop, slugs, my mother, thunder and nuclear threat. Is this a life? We press on.

OLD PERSONS

I have been grovelling through my old photos searching for pictures of my youth. I find one of myself and chums sitting on a lawn playing bongos, saxophone, balalaika and recorder. Very hip, I feel. Daughter and her chum can't see why. To them we are wearing normal clothes. I admit I am playing a drippy recorder, but hang on! I am wearing drainpipes! And this was Ruislip 1959, when denim, needlecord and bongos were cutting edge.

We were really wild. And then I gave up shoes. Neighbours, relatives and the conductress on the 49 bus were outraged. Even Daughter is impressed. No shoes on the tubes and buses! All this sickening nostalgia is welling up because of my looming sixtieth birthday and Elvis is everywhere again. How he brings it all back: the screaming and swooning, the rock and roll, the cross-patch parents. Those parents didn't know their luck. We had parties with barely any sex, drink or drugs.

Daughter is horrified. What sort of parties were they? Yesterday she returned home at 8 a.m. after a thrilling night of clubbing, free champagne and outrageous behaviour. She gives cheery impressions of being fearfully drunk. I feel compelled to mention liver damage and ruin her fun. I am turning into my mother.

Meanwhile my mother is still being my mother. She has forbidden me to have a party. I've invited too many people, the house is too small, where will she go, how will she sleep?

'Your mother is worried to death about this party!' says the home-care lady after my mother's bath. The two of them have been in that bathroom scaring each other witless. They see a house crammed with drink- and drug-crazed guests, its walls bulging, roaring music, deranged gatecrashers and house-trashers pouring in from lower

Holloway. And all I wanted to do was to re-live my charming youth for one evening, in period costume.

But wait. In my youth, my mother was in charge. Things were not charming at all. Neighbourhood spies reported on my parties, friends were reprimanded and banned, outfits were mocked, Elvis was scorned. My youth was obviously crap. And now Fielding has just seen the photo. 'That picture, by any contemporary standards, is sad,' says he strictly. 'The fact that you ran around barefoot does not make you Timothy Leary.' Shall I invite him or not?

COLON CONSCIOUS

Gardener's chum rings with news of his colon. He has given it a thorough clean-out over the weekend. For two whole days he has swallowed nothing but aloe vera juice and colon-cleansing pills. Thank goodness. This is a fellow who for years has eaten three hamburgers for luncheon. How does he still have a functioning colon at all?

But it just shows how the world is changing. In the new Global Village, bowels are centre stage. We are obsessed with food and dying of consumption, the new kind, i.e. three hamburgers for lunch. Or nothing for lunch. What a world! Some of us waddling around busting with fat, others starving to death, some stuffing any old crap, others mimsying about with health foods, and Gardener's chum is one of the new crossovers. This has been a sort of barrier weekend for him – behind it were the rubbish years, before he knew about food. Post barrier will be health food only and a lovely clean, pink colon.

My mother could do with one of those. She's had a hell of a time with her colon, but to be fair, it is nearly a hundred years old. Now it is in charge of her life. She thinks of little else and is only happy when it's empty. Recently she has begged for enemas, a brutal treatment at her age. This is the downside of eating and colon problems in our house: my mother likes to share them.

So I am sick of food, cooking and bowels. If, for a heavenly moment, I manage to forget the endless food palaver, some reminder is bound to crop up: a cookery programme, my mother's reflux, Nigella's new book, the dog's colitis, a new poison warning, the latest grisly obesity figures.

Fielding saw more food news on telly: 'The average American is clinically obese.' Or panicking in the gym. When we were young, we

195

ate blithely. We grew up with barely a food thought. 'I just refuelled,' said Fielding. 'I went to the woods, ran around, came back famished and ate white bread and jam and Battenberg cake.' If he eats such things now, his family screams with fright and plies him with Quorn. Paradise for him is football on telly and a thick wodge of pig-sausage sandwich with brown sauce. Secretly he knows that the Arsenal team have a dietician each. Help!

HEALTHY DIET

Apparently the tea dances in eighteenth-century Bath were not as delightful as they're cracked up to be. When the assembled company rose en masse to rush to the tea table, the stench caused one contemporary observer to fall down in a dead faint. He referred to the dancers as so many 'rotting human bellows'.

This description fits me to a T now that I am on the way downhill. I suspect many of the tea dancers were mature persons whose innards were beginning to play them up. As one gets older, this sort of problem seems to get worse. The stomach bloats and blocks up and one wanders around like a barrage balloon, unable to bend in the middle, so sitting at table, in restaurants, theatres and cinemas becomes something of an ordeal. At least this is my personal experience. I tend to stay at home, where I can lie flat on the floor when necessary.

But flicking through a health cookery book, I notice a cure for bloated abdomens filled with putrefaction and blocked gases. Our prayers are answered! I throw away the chip pan and whack my mother on to a health diet of fennel à la Grèque, tabbouleh with mint and parsley, organic potatoes and a little delicately grilled fish. Soon it will all be gliding through her happy bowels, unimpeded.

She is furious and stabs at her plate. 'These aren't cooked, this has no bloody taste and this stinks,' she cries. 'It's all going down the lavatory!' Just wait. Tomorrow she'll be forcefed globe artichokes, cabbage and plums for irritability and anger.

My friend Fielding is also opposed to health food. The staff in his local health shop are no incentive. 'One's a mountain, one's a matchstick and the other talks rubbish,' he shouts offensively, still smarting from the forty-eight-hour fruit diet his wife ordered to stop him

197

turning to suet. For two days he shivered and lived mainly in the lavatory and then collapsed with flu, but only gained more weight, because he had sneaked downstairs at midnight and eaten whole pounds of cheese.

Now my builder tells me of his mate's diet. Nothing for breakfast, an apple for lunch, then half a pound of butter on his potatoes at supper, plus three avocados and a bedtime snack the size of your average person's daily intake.

Fortunately, tea dances have faded out.

WHY PARTY?

Why does one have parties? Thank heavens mine is over. It's the run up to the thing that tends to wreck it: the weeks of planning, expense, organising and my mother panicking. Will she collapse with fright on the day?

'I'm going to die straight after your party,' says she rather dramatically. She promises to try and hang on until it's all over, but will she manage it? And there are other worries: will so-and-so be rude to X because they're still friends with somebody she loathes. Will my mother shout at Y and Z, who displeased her in the distant past. She has not forgotten their crimes and now has decades of pent-up bile, ready to bust out the minute the hated guests appear. And she is not the only one waiting and fuming. All these little festering feuds threaten our evening.

And isn't it odd that however carefully one plans party day, it always speeds up, with the last few hours whizzing past like greased lightning, so that nothing is quite ready as one approaches blast-off. Daughter is still fiddling with the garden fairy lights, Gardener is still soldering wires for the hi-fi, none of the snacks are ready, the hot water has run out and I cannot find my party frock. And my mother's special cheesy thing, which tasted heavenly in last week's practice run, now tastes weird and we have made it in industrial quantities.

Then comes that first bleak hour when no one has arrived yet, except the few people I don't know very well, who have no one to talk to. Fielding is two hours late, and he promised absolutely to be here, on time, chatting skilfully. This is when I sit on the floor crying and wish and wish that I had just had a takeaway and video at home with the dog.

Too late, the ball is rolling, we must carry on. I turn to drink, the dog is cracking up, my mother is calming down, the guests are flooding in, they form little groups, they seem to be speaking, some of them are dancing, so why shouldn't I? It is, after all, my party. I can have a dance and scream if I want to, so I do that for the last two hours. I have rather a wild time. I think I enjoyed myself. I hope everyone else did.

DILDO AWARENESS MONTH

This seems to be dildo awareness month. I have seen several on telly recently, mostly in that lesbian romp on a Wednesday. What a ghastly thing to see, especially while sitting next to one's mother. I left the room pretty sharpish. My mother remained glaring at the screen entranced. When one is ninety-six, it must be gripping to see all these ex-secret things on your own telly.

But I am fairly sick of dildos. Last week we saw pink wiggly ones and gleaming leather ones, and my friend Jean's mother was given one for her birthday. She waved it about shamelessly at table. And in the summer a visitor left three in my airing cupboard. She thought I might like to use them. She had perhaps forgotten that I am a repressed person riddled with guilt and shame. A dildo is my least favourite object. And what if my mother had come across them? Not that there's anything wrong with widdling about with a dildo, but must the whole family be told?

And how accurate is the telly portrayal? My friend Munch, a lesbian, assures me that she and her chums rarely charge about with dildos and pans of warm milk. Anyway, who wants to know? I suspect that blokes do. Fielding does, for a start. He was glued to the lesbian drama – briefly. But then he felt rather agitated and changed channels to watch perfectly formed men playing football – another sort of gay romp – and found that he much preferred it. He has also taken a particular fancy to Johnny Depp.

'People talk a lot of nonsense about the sexual divide,' said he bossily and droned on about the spectrum of sexuality. My dog is all over the spectrum, and obviously so is Fielding, after weeks of dildo saturation. On Thurday there was liberated staff room chat about the wretched things. Fielding hid in a corner. Now he has just returned from Sweden, where he attended a talk by Catherine M. It was packed out with men. Fielding and his chum went along for literary and philosophical reasons. In their opinion Catherine looked as if she hadn't been near any genitalia, real or pretend, for heaven knows how long. They had a couple of beers and agreed that she needed a jolly good seeing-to. Dildo awareness month is getting us nowhere.

THE QUEEN OF TACT

Olga came round in one of her favourite jumpers which she'd found in an Oxfam shop. It was brightly coloured, decades old, hand-knitted and the wool slightly matted with age, but Olga loved it and, as she is an artist, she knew it was beautiful.

My mother was horrified. She rummaged desperately in her cupboards and hauled out all her old jumpers, fluffy mohair and knitted by herself and begged Olga to take one. 'It's better than that thing,' she said in her forthright way, pointing at Olga's beloved woolly. Luckily Olga was very keen on my mother's offering. She is to have it shortly for her birthday.

'I wouldn't wipe the floor with the one *she* was wearing,' said my mother later. Perhaps she is learning tact. She kept this final damning critique until after Olga had left. This was no mean feat for my mother. She usually sees tact as an untruth. If someone looks a fright, then she *must* tell them. 'But suppose they don't want to know?' I ask. Tough. My mother cannot lie.

'You've got a fat bum,' she called out last week, seeing me outlined in a long pink vest.

'It's the pink,' I shouted, ripped it off and put on a black one. But then I foolishly wore some baggy trousers.

'Your bum is definitely getting fatter,' cried my mother again, and then she advised me to buy a wig. She is on a roll. Spotting Rosemary and I trudging off for our dog walk, she felt a need to blurt the truth again.

'You both look *schlumperdich*!' she called. I translated for Rosemary. Drudgy. This is nothing new. My mother has often nagged Rosemary. 'Why d'you wear those dark colours?' she has moaned on. 'They do nothing for your complexion. You need a bit of colour!'

Rosemary doesn't even own a lipstick. My mother can scarcely move without one.

Last night Rosemary and I sat in her living room looking plain. 'I'm not attractive,' said Rosemary in a heart-rending way.

'You are!' I shouted, *and* Rosemary is saintly. After all this she *still* admires my mother. 'She's marvellous. So smart. She must have looked stunning in her youth,' says Rosemary like a disciple. She paused for a moment. 'Will you buy me a lipstick for Christmas?'

Can my mother's harsh strategy be working?

XMAS PLANS

Rosemary has a bizarre plan for Christmas. She will cook the turkey at home and then drive it miles out into the sticks to her sister's home for the festive lunch. What? Is she mad? Why don't the family come to Rosemary's place? Better still, why doesn't her sister cook the turkey? But Rosemary springs to her sister's defence. 'She's a vegetarian! She can't cook a corpse!'

Pooh! What a weedy excuse. I am also a vegetarian. All those stories of dangling conveyor-belt chickens having their heads sliced off and the tortured pigs and the shit-eating sheep and cattle finally did it for me. Yet I must still cook the annual corpse. But not this year. I have a reprieve. Hurrah! Daughter has decided to cook the turkey, now that she has her own home to do it in. My mother and I may go there for dinner. What bliss for me. No sweating over the cooker and stuffing.

But can my mother relax? Not a hope in hell. She is now pretty sure that this really has to be her Last Christmas (the eighth Last Christmas) and still no one has written down her famous stuffing recipe, neither Daughter nor I have paid proper attention to the method and this is our very last chance to learn it. Or it would have been, but if Daughter does the dinner the stuffing recipe will be lost for ever. Panic stations as usual.

My mother is making odd signs. She draws rectangles in the air. What can she mean? The wretched aphasia is concealing some vital information. Then more frantic gestures. Yes! These are stuffing gestures. And the rectangles must be vacuum-packed whole cooked chestnuts. How do I know this? Months of practice. My mother is thrilled to have got the message across. I must buy chestnuts, we must make the stuffing, then all Daughter will have to do is shove it in. Will she manage? My mother is on tenterhooks.

But not for long. Daughter won't have to manage. She's changed her mind. She can't be fagged to do all that. I can do it. Then she and her chum Rae can come over and eat it, so can the Italian lodgers, so can Gardener on his return from his mother's and so can the dog. I will now be catering for eight instead of nought. Stuffed again.

CONSTIPATION

At last the Incontinence Lady visits to check on my mother's condition and find out whether she needs the mountain of incontinence pads piling up in our basement. Because my mother is not incontinent at all. She's just scared stiff that one day she will be and we will be unprepared, so she must stockpile these things and often wear them day and night, just in case her bladder and bowels suddenly lose their grip on things.

Usually they have too tight a grip, so the talk turns to constipation. What a treat for my mother. Now that she is very old, her bottom often preys on her mind. When one is lying in bed, bored sick by the telly and too exhausted to read, it is difficult not to consider one's body, especially if part of it is clogged with toxic cement. But who can my mother share her bottom thoughts with? Only me. Most people tend to mock or shy away from this topic. And there are times: meal times, or times when I am feeling artistic or sensitive, when even I recoil from bowel talk. Now, at last, here is someone happy to chat about blockages in a robust and upbeat way.

The Incontinence Lady understands. She knows why this ailment can fill your every waking thought, and better still, she knows that things can be even worse than we suspected. She has constipation stories to make the jaw drop. She even silences my mother – a rare power. We both sit, gaping and speechless.

This is an ailment, says our visitor, that can kill if you refuse to deal with it. 'It can back up to here!' says she, pointing at her chest, 'and then . . . ' The rest is too frightful to relate, but my mother and I scream with a ghastly sort of excitement. Rosemary's sister, a nurse in the fifties and sixties, confirms these tales of horror. Lie in bed all day without drinking quite enough, and you're done for.

So my mother must drinks gallons of water daily, which means running to the lavatory all night. She is infuriated. There is no peace for the constipated. For those in the opposite camp there is at least some consolation, says Fielding. 'Elvis the King wore nappies at Vegas!' But my mother doesn't give a shit. She couldn't anyway.

TOUGH WEEK

This week my mother wants to die more than ever, the dog is vomiting blood, American Cousin is crippled with a searing mystery pain and we are at war. What a struggle it is to have a laugh and relax. Fielding's week has also been gruesome, what with teaching, the vicious toothache and Arsenal out of Europe. To escape the ghastliness of life for an hour or so, he went to the pictures and saw *The Hours*. Compared to our level of aggro, he thought Virginia Woolf's problems rather mimsy. 'It's a bit rarified,' said he. 'She should try a fifty/fifty tackle with Roy Keane.'

How ever is one to keep cheery? We are slogging away at it, trying all methods, even laughter-yoga groups, but are they worth the bother? Olga's yoga isn't working. She's been at it week after week, for years and years and she still hasn't mellowed out. Last week she arrived at her class, couldn't find her newly purchased yoga season ticket, and no one would let her in, even though they had the transaction on record. So Olga had a frightful tantrum and screamed at the manager. And guess what? He screamed back. Even here, in a venue devoted to relaxation, everyone is ready to blow a gasket.

'I'm sick of the lot of you!' roared the manager. 'You think you're so cosmic, well you're not! You're just a bunch of brain-dead hippies who took too many drugs in the sixties!' And with that, he closed the whole yoga class down. All Olga's fault. Now poor Daughter has discovered that the charming little house she is renting and thought was a converted brick factory, is in fact a converted morgue. Human bones have been exhumed in the foundations. It was already rather grisly over there, minutes from murder mile. Daughter suspects that there are ghouls and ghosties hanging around her bedroom. And like the rest of us, she had been searching for reasons to be cheerful.

But where has Gardener been all this time? Far away on the Internet, searching for impeccable news sources. Here he comes, waving some papers. He has compiled a concise but fiercely accurate summary of what's going on in the war, with complementary reading list. 'I advise you to read this,' says he strictly. Oh, thank you so very much.

REVENGE OF THE FLUFFIES

We have moved my mother's bedroom around so that her bed is alongside the window. She may now lie there gazing out upon the wonderland that is spring. Fabulous. She adores those swanky magpies from the tree next door and the dinky, fluffy squirrels. Nobody else does. Gardener longs to chase the bullying magpies away and Rosemary is entrenched in bitter conflict with the squirrels.

'They come dancing and twirling along the branches,' shouts Rosemary, 'they see a lovely new shoot, wrench it off, bite it to bits and throw it on the ground.' Goodbye horse chestnut buds and camellias and almost goodbye Rosemary. The spray she squirted up into the branches – 'extremely distasteful and irritant to squirrels' – blew straight back and poured into her mouth. She had failed to read the label, which warned that persons with breathing difficulties, like herself, should not use this vicious spray.

The squirrels just sat munching and gloating at Rosemary as she almost choked to death. And what mayhem over in Sylvia's garden! The pestilential squirrels have trashed her lilies and sweet peas, which are trussed up in netting, but Sylvia swears she's seen them untying the knots. They are so brazen. Like the bird-killer hedgehogs of Uist and our rats down here in town. While shopping in Waltham Cross, my friend Dave spotted sixteen rats in two hours, sauntering around squeaking. Same as the rats in our park which stroll about waiting for snacks, ignoring traps and swim about trailing Weil's disease across the ponds.

But Fielding's spring battle is with himself, because it's not only the little fluffy creatures that are out creating havoc, it's women without their coats on. Now the weather is hotting up, they're all out and about in their T-shirts. Fielding spotted several coatless women in clingy, strappy, off-the-shoulder numbers in the health food shop and had to run outside in a sweat. Being a sensitive fellow, he can't help but appreciate spring. He sees the world aflame, burnished; he feels lyrical, but also desperately needs to play more and more intense, bosom-free footer.

What a difficult age this is, all battles and turmoil. Old enough to go pointlessly wild, not old enough to give up. Watch out for the next TV series: *sixtysomething*. For once my mother is at an advantage. She can only lie back and watch the carnage in peace.

MOBILE ADVERTS

I open the front door and see a desperate figure. Is that the first Mrs Rochester standing screaming and wailing at the top of the stairs in her nightie with her hair awry? No. It is my poor mother in a panic. Where have I been, why am I so late, she thought I was dead! But how, on a dog walk? Easy, thinks my mother: crashed on the way home, drowned in a pond, gobbled up by Rottweilers. She is the Anxiety Queen on overdrive. She knows that if there is a psychopath on the loose, he is bound to home in on her only child.

She cannot help this. It runs in the family. I do it myself when Daughter goes off the radar, but luckily Daughter has a mobile. That has to be the answer. I must get one, programme my number into my mother's phone and she will be able to send out a mayday call at the touch of one button. Even the news of this plan soothes her. She is happy, but I feel rather glum. I must break my vow never to have a ghastly mobile.

I hate the pesky things. Remember that horrid advert in which the poor unfashionable mobile falls from a table? It is unattractive, isolated, unloved and probably seriously injured, but what happens? Everybody laughs themselves sick. Who would want to approve such callous behaviour and buy such a product?

Returning from York on the train Rosemary saw just how the mobile phone aids wickedness. A drunken soldier on leave borrowed his chum's mobile to phone three women and line them up for three consecutive bonking opportunities that very night, the last one being his wife, who he advised not to wait up. 'The train's delayed,' he lied, when really it was just pulling into Euston.

So goodbye moral standards and resolutions, I am off to buy a mobile. Within hours I own one of the little horrors. I take it on our walk. Soon I am bellowing into it, just like all those people I have mocked for years. 'Hello! I'm still on the Heath, we're having a coffee, back in half an hour.' My mother is relaxing in heaven but Rosemary is scarlet with shame.

'Marvellous,' I say, overexcited. 'That's calmed her down.'

'D'you know what you just said?' snaps Rosemary. 'You said marvellous!'

'Did I?'

CHOKING TO DEATH. NEARLY

Round comes my mother's birthday again, the ninety-seventh, and we are off to the favourite Chinese restaurant. Same again but more of a cliff-hanger than ever, because my mother has a terrifying new ailment – sudden choking. It started, in a milder form, a year or so ago as she laughed herself almost sick at Ethel's funeral service on *EastEnders*. I must say I thought her rather callous. I was having a quiet little cry and there was my mother bent double on her chair, mocking Dot's torment and hymn-singing. Unwisely, she laughed while eating her dinner and nearly choked to death. That would have been just her luck, to die laughing at a TV funeral.

Now how are we to relax at meal times? Last night we had a pre-birthday outing with Cousins to a Greek restaurant. Rashly, my mother chose lamb. Suddenly she was in difficulties. It could have been one of two problems – chewing or choking. We couldn't quite make out which. The Cousins went rather pale, but luckily it was the chewing – rated as amber alert only. My mother bravely battled on with her dinner, in weeny mouthfuls only.

She is not the only one battling. Rosemary's mother also choked in a Chinese restaurant. The whole family froze, but luckily a bevy of Chinese waiters rushed out and ministered to her in a loving way, stood her up, sat her down, patted her, provided iced water. 'We realised how useless we English were,' said Rosemary, ashamed. Now their outings are always knife edge, because Rosemary's mother threatens to choke. 'I mustn't choke, dear,' says she, switching everyone to panic stations.

What luck that Gardener's sister, a nurse, was present at last year's Christmas dinner, when his mother started quietly coughing and going pink. No one quite caught on. We had a suspicion that something was amiss, but sat like lummoxes, thinking vaguely of Heimlich's manoeuvre, when up jumped the sister and did it. Phew. So we are all practising the manoeuvre like mad.

But why give up our restaurant outings? Staying in doing nothing can be even more risky. Not so long ago my mother had a terrible choke while laughing at *Morecambe and Wise*, even without a crumb of food in her mouth. We now know what the last laugh means. 'Don't get old!' wails my mother poignantly. If only.

CELLO

I am having my cello lesson. Bliss. One hour's escape from the daily drear. I rush upstairs for some money to pay Teacher, but what is wrong with my mother? She has her hands clapped over her ears, is wailing loudly and wearing a look of pain.

'You're not to pay her!' she roars, incensed that Teacher is to be rewarded for her part in the ghastly cello playing. But Teacher and I ignore this critique. We know that I will never be Jacqueline du Pré. My practice is minimal, the tone often grating and growling, the tuning wambly, but sometimes, just sometimes, I manage a few pleasant bars, which makes my years of struggle worth it.

If only I had learnt this divine instrument decades ago, instead of now, with the elderly stick fingers, failing eyesight and the brain stymied by the tenor clef. But my dream is to play, before I peg out, in a small orchestra. And another dream – to play Fats Domino-style piano, accompanied by anyone else who cares to join in. Quick, before we all get arthritis.

This is the big cloud hanging over my plan. Decrepitude and inca-pacity may catch up with me before I make it. How many baroque gems will I never have time to play or even hear? How fluent will my sight-reading never be, now that the Last Big Deadline is looming. So I must practise like billy-o, despite fierce opposition.

Last week in the broiling heat, I practised the cello with the French windows open. Daughter, sunbathing in the garden with chums, begged me to shut the door, or practise the piano instead. So I did. More wailing from my mother upstairs.

But their suffering and my efforts are paying off. Last week I played in a small orchestra, easy bits only, but what a divine inter-lude. Join an orchestra, forget the world.

How sensible of me to have forced Daughter to learn the violin as a child. She can now play it. We try some simple duets. Soon we hear the dreaded rumbling of my mother's stairlift. She descends, she glares, and then – surprise of the century – she applauds! 'First time I've heard you sound nice,' says she. But I musn't be bitter. She is *being positive* – a new skill! We can all have one, even at ninety-seven. Next week – 'Blueberry Hill'.

ON HEAT

Bad luck. Just as I was planning a heavenly week swimming daily in the broiling heat – snap! Something nasty happened to my spine. Then, as I lay crippled on the sofa, my mother recklessly flopped into her reclining armchair. Horrors. She could not un-recline it. The front bit wouldn't go down again. Imagine the pathetic scene: my mother wedged like a Kafka beetle into her chair and me with my cracking back, unable to haul her out of it.

Luckily I was able to drag the pull-youself-off-the-lavatory frame to the armchair and my mother managed to prise herself free. This is the bonus to having a real cripple in the house. We have handy contraptions that I may commandeer, now that my back has gone for a burton: the pick-up pincer stick, the stairlift, the bathlift, and the Zimmer frame for dog walks – a grim taste of things to come.

Then Rosemary rushed round with a portable folding seat for back support. What a saint. I stuck it in the car, drove off for some petrol and there was the poor garage man, also lumbering about with a wrecked spine. Apparently backs go to hell in the heat, so do railtracks, tempers and teeth. Fielding was suddenly clobbered by a murderous toothache last week, but Dentist only blamed the heat.

As he staggered home racked with pain, Fielding observed a violent altercation between some overheated male motorists. They were perhaps unaccustomed to sweating and being boiled alive. I, on the other hand, am used to it, being stuck in what seems to be a nine-year menopause. I am on a fairly permanent rolling boil. What heat wave? Can't tell the difference. So, hey girls! Why not forget HRT, now that it's even more scary? Just stick to the menopause and have your own personal, endless, tropical summer.

Because one may as well be positive about these things. The roasting heat is helping us all to relax. People are far less inhibited. It is now permissable to rip your clothes off when out and about. Naked ramblers stride about the woods and dales. Around the ponds on our Heath the lawns are piled with nearly nude persons, sunbathing, exercising, puffing, snogging, squirming and grilling. It's the sixties all over again. Remember them? The sex, drugs and rock and roll? And best of all, our lovely bendy spines. Aaaah!

WALKIES WITH THE GRIM REAPER

My mother wakes in a desolate mood. 'I'm waiting to die,' says she weedily. It's a grim wait if you are prone to anxiety. My poor mother has been awake since 4 a.m. worrying about her jewellery. What will happen to it when she's gone? Will I wear the bracelets? Will I lose them, forget them, sell them, be ripped off, mugged while wearing them? By 9 a.m. she has worked herself into a frenzy.

Time for a diversion, so Rosemary and I trundle her out in the wheelchair for a dog walkie. Soon we are among the Sunday morning crowds – sun shining, children playing on their little bicycles, the dog pouncing on its squeaky ball, swans gliding across the pond, yuccas in flower, live persons playing tennis. My mother is enchanted. Briefly. But then, for some odd reason, Rosemary will keep mentioning death.

'Let's look at my friend's mother's memorial bench,' says she, shoving the wheelchair towards it. Rosemary reads out the heart-rending inscription. Quick, swivel my mother round so she can look at rolling hills and a stunningly attractive tree turning orange.

'Autumn!' moans Rosemary, 'season of decay. The summer is over.' Thank heavens for the dog. It throws its squeaky into my mother's lap. We have a laugh, but not for long. The Grim Reaper is glooming along on our walk. Rosemary is thinking of death again and talking of her poor friend who is dying in a hospice, aged only sixty-three and no one dares ask about funerals. So Rosemary must plan her own now. She must be sprinkled half over her husband, please, and half somewhere else, she isn't quite sure where.

Who can blame Rosemary for droning about death? This is a grim time of life for us: remaining parents and even friends are fading away, old age is looming. Suddenly we are in a rush, trying to pack things in before we peg out. I'm going back to school and Rosemary is going to Brazil, which means she must learn Portuguese. 'I met a rather handsome man on the train yesterday,' says she, forgetting about death for a while. 'He spoke Portuguese.'

Our walk is nearly over. We reach the car. 'This car is a shithole!' shouts my mother.

'Disgusting!' shouts Rosemary, ganging up. 'I don't know why she can't clean it.' Back to normal. Our walkie has worked a treat.

MICROWAVE HELL

We have a gas leak, the oven must be turned off and, of the few remaining suitably qualified plumbers still alive in England, none are available for days on end. Thank heavens we have the microwave. But I have not yet mastered it. I can only heat things up.

'Don't be pathetic!' snaps Rosemary. 'I've cooked on a microwave for months. I have the best microwave cook book.' She produces it. What rubbish this book is. 'Cook your pasta the conventional way,' it says. Oh, thank you. With what? Never mind. We'll have potatoes. But wait. One needs an advanced maths degree to cope with this ghastly bit of equipment.

All portions are for four, two or one, in litres and grams and 'oven wattages range from 500 to 780', says Rosemary's book. No they don't. Ours is 850. And there are three of us, our scales are in pounds and ounces and I still speak in pints. Imagine the translation. If it's 8–9 minutes for 575 g for four at 100 per cent power at 500-780 watts, what is it in lb and oz for three at 850?

Out comes Delia's conversion page, the microwave instructions, paper and pencil for sums, and all this on top of my normal struggle to follow a recipe and remember instructions. I read one: '2tsp. sugar,' but by the time I've reached the sugar, two seconds later, the instruction has vanished. The brain is empty. What spnfls were they? Tspns? Tblspns? Haven't a clue. Back to the book. Tspsns. And what number gas? Forgotten. Back to the book. And if someone speaks while the brain is carrying the instruction across the kitchen, then poof! It's gone again. Back to the book. How many miles have I travelled in this kitchen? How many tempers have I lost?

At least a microwave makes the cooking quicker. Says who? You need a great pile of microwaves, because with only one, everything must be cooked separately, then goes cold, then is reheated, then tastes like poop.

Hours later we have a dull dinner. 'Very nice,' says Gardener stoically, but leaves his pappy vegetables almost untouched. Why? Because a) it's taken so long that he's snacked heavily while waiting, and b) they have nil taste. Upstairs my mother is showering hers with salt, increasing the risk of heart attack and another stroke. A gas explosion might have been safer.

ORAL SEX

I find my mother in bed stabbing at a back copy of the newspaper with her finger. She is in a roaring bate. What ever is the matter?

'Canni langi,' she shouts crossly. 'Canni langi!' Does she want pasta for lunch? No. This is aphasic for oral sex. My poor mother keeps coming across it everywhere. Of course she's heard of it before, she knew about Monica and the President, but things are hotting up now. Shockingly detailed information has begun to penetrate even the shelter of my mother's bedroom, via the papers and telly chat shows — about the Turner Prize, that Meg Ryan film, the plaguey Internet, so my poor mother now has oral sex stuck in her head. She would prefer flower paintings.

So would I, but we are out of luck. And worst of all, with the talk of blow jobs and canni langi, comes talk of my mother's least favourite thing: pubic hair. Even a single tiny stray one can cause uproar in our house, but now my mother hears that entire front bottoms are to be visible at the public cinema. Horrifying news.

Fielding, like my mother, is also lagging behind the times. He was surprised to find that oral sex, particularly the very popular blowjob, is now called foreplay. So was I. We had always thought of it as right-at-the-very-end-play, even post-end-play, yards after number ten, and only for the very adventurous or seriously in love. We cannot get to grips with the new revisionist view, which places the blow-job on a level with the daily tea break.

But Olivia is managing to go with the flow. 'It's so handy,' says she. 'You can do it anywhere: in a train, in offices, in a car. Americans do masses of it at summer camps.' She has a point, and we must applaud those Americans. This is, after all, one of the rare forms of safe sex allowed to religious maniacs. We don't mind, we're liberal-minded, so long as news of it isn't being pumped into my mother's bedroom day and night.

When Fielding embarked upon a romance in his youth, the nearest he got to Emily Dunlop was seventy yards. Further progress was slow, oral sex was nowhere. Now it is everywhere. Some of us are sick to death of it, but what about Fielding? Where is he tonight, by the way? At the cinema!

SQUABBLES

Rosemary and I tried to cooperate over the cooking last night. We found each other very annoying.

'I have a wonderful recipe for spare ribs,' shouted Rosemary excitedly. 'I'm doing it tonight.' What a coincidence. I was also planning spare ribs with red cabbage, so I asked her for the recipe.

'I'm not telling,' she snapped. 'It won't go with red cabbage.' Naturally I argued and begged for the recipe. If I wish to make my household sick with two conflicting recipes, then that is my affair. Eventually Rosemary gave in. She would cook double quantity and give me half. What a saint! But then she fell asleep in the afternoon and was late preparing the marinade, which threw our whole schedule out. If my mother's dinner is served later than 7.30 p.m. it plays havoc with her digestion and she will be up half the night moaning with pain and Rosemary will become a hate figure.

I had to wake Rosemary and tell her to get on with it. She was resentful, but knowing what was at stake, she carried on, and our dinner was a roaring success, if rather sickly. But this communal cooking was harrowing and does not bode well for our elderly commune. I see now why collectives are difficult to run.

My friend Fielding, who has experienced collective living, tells me that they tend to have purges. 'The majority gangs up against some poor hapless bastard, who is then exiled from the collective.'

This seems to be happening in my mother's bridge circle. At ninety-seven, rather impressively, she has just embarked on a new social whirl of bridge afternoons, but unfortunately, has found fault with a fellow bridge player. This lady *will* criticise my mother's sugar intake and stretches her legs out under the table in a selfish way, leaving no room for anyone else. Naturally my mother gave her a kick and is stirring up discontent among the players. Imagine my mother in charge of a collective.

Rosemary and are aiming for a rather more laid-back approach. Despite our catering squabble we have not given up the idea, and I personally have my eye on the ruins of Friern Barnet Hospital. It has everything: a main building (with potential for dance hall, jacuzzi and swimming pool), outlying chalets, and huge grounds for gardening and farming. Anyone arguing over the marinade could be hustled off to a locked ward.

THE NEW WALKER

In the summer, being rather poorly, Rosemary's mother returned from living in the USA, where there is no National Health, but where the walkers (Zimmers with wheels, we call them) are of a fabulously high standard. They have brakes, seats, shopping baskets and cost an arm and a leg. Mother brought her beloved walker home with her.

Then tragedy. The walker broke. Rosemary and I toured London in the boiling summer sun, looking for a close replica. We found one, Rosemary drove it to her mother, who was bitterly disappointed. It just wasn't good enough. Rosemary schlepped it back to the shop, found another one, and catalogues, ferried them to her mother again, who rejected everything out of hand.

Then came a gap in the storyline. Rosemary would not talk about it. I would say 'Walker,' tears would come to her eyes, she grabbed for the cigarettes and started shouting. The sight of my mother, with her common NHS walker, made Rosemary cry buckets. Now the story has picked up again. A kind friend in the USA is tracking down the exact walker from the exact shop in the same backwoods town in which the original walker was purchased. E-mails between Rosemary and the friend have been whizzing back and forth across the pond, with ghastly reports of raging forest fires, charred wastelands, deaths of friends, funerals, but always, always, news of the walker must come first. The friend will bring it to London. Rosemary has gone on strike.

Rosemary's mother does not know her luck. Towards the end of her life, Fielding's mother bypassed walkers and went straight into a standard English wheelchair. One of her poor old legs, rotten with ulcers, had to be amputated. 'I haven't a leg to stand on,' said she, having a bitter laugh. Fielding loved his mummy. He shoved her all over Buckinghamshire, but her pain grew worse, her drugs stronger and her chat duller, so he pushed her on ever more adventurous outings. He became the Thierry Henry of wheelchair pushers, almost cavalier, left his mother outside the sweetshop, forgot the brakes, and off she rolled into the jeweller's. 'Fucking idiot!' his mother cried, polite all her life but made desperate by events.

'It's all coming our way,' shouts Fielding in a panic. 'Be nice to your children. They'll be pushing your wheelchair.' And selecting your nursing home. And providing your walker.

WET, WET, WET

What a dreary week. Our home is Bleak House inside out. Drip, drip. The dog has wet the bed and sofa repeatedly, my mother has possible cystitis and I dare not cough or sneeze, just in case. The bathroom bin is crammed with nappies, the radiators swathed in drying sheets, the duvets have been lugged to the cleaners. Outside the ceaseless rain pours down, the car sun-roof is leaking, the lawn a quagmire. We are mopping up inside and out.

At midnight I hear someone crashing about in the bathroom. Who can it be? It is my desperate mother, crazed with panic, blundering and crawling about trying to scrub the lavatory and entire bathroom floor. She is terrified of noxious smells and loss of bladder control, and who can blame her? What hellish future is she looking at, swaddled in nappies and shunned by visitors?

I beg her to stop the grim cleaning. There is not the slightest odour, I swear it. Our bathroom smells clearly of lavender – and Dettol and aqua descaler and pine floor cleaner. I know because I have been on red alert, scrubbing, spraying and rinsing in there since the first weeny hint of smell threatened our happiness.

Luckily things calm down after only two days of terror. My mother stops tottering to the lavatory, the dog regains control of its bladder, all risk of stink has gone and we begin to live again.

What havoc the bladder can cause. It ruined the last few years of Fielding's mother's life. She was always fond of a laugh, but her bladder put paid to that. She forbade Fielding to crack any more amusing jokes, because with every laugh came a leak.

'God's last little joke,' says Fielding bitterly, remembering his darling mummy, po-faced in her monster nappies and knickers, unable to laugh, cough or sneeze. He issues a terrible warning. 'Do THOSE

EXERCISES NOW.' Being a shy fellow he cannot say 'cervical floor'.

But Sylvia and I have been doing them for years because we knew this might happen. We find that they are not 100 per cent reliable. Meanwhile Sylvia's dog has also lost control of its bladder. It is banned from its favourite sofa and must sit glumly on plastic. At least Sylvia can barely smell a thing. That faculty faded away years ago. We would normally have had a laugh about all this, but do we dare?

THE HOIST

Last week my mother slid off the bed and wrenched her poorly arthritic knee. It is impossible to lift a whole mother off the floor, so I screamed for help. Gardener and I hauled my mother on to the bed like a beached whale.

Then what? Pretty soon the big problem reared up. How was my mother to get to the lavatory without standing? Round came the doctor, who alerted the social services, who came running round in droves: with relays of carers, therapists, team leader, district nurse, a commode, bedpan and a hoist. My poor mother must be hauled up and down like a sack of turnips.

What a nightmare this ghastly contraption is, but much better than bedpans and nappies, so I am given a hoist lesson: slide this bit of slippery harness down the back, put these bits under the legs, cross these straps over, hook them on to this, don't bang her head on that, press the button and we have lift-off. There goes my mother, dangling and screeching in the air and swinging across to her destination the commode. Imagine us fiddling about with all this at 3 a.m. or at dawn when our wits are rather dull.

My mother has a dinging bell to whack when she needs hoisting. Ding, ding! Our lives revolve round the lavatory. We always thought they did, but now they really do. 'Don't get old,' croaks my mother, dangling from the yellow harness. What a ghastly glimpse of things to come for me and the Daughter. The hoist awaits us all.

'Will you be like this, Mum?' asks Daughter, a touch apprehensive. This is the trouble with having one's mother to stay. The whole truth is out about old age. Nothing works, nothing tastes pleasant, bits decay, other bits hurt. No wonder my mother is sinking into silence and gloom. She can barely be fagged to eat or speak.

But meanwhile, here is a hymn of praise to social services and the NHS. What saints they all are. Day after day the pairs of carers whirl in, efficient, glamorous, upbeat, even amusing. Soon I hear my mother having a laugh. They are partying up in her bedroom. And why not? Nothing is broken, the fat knee is shrinking and within days my mother has spurned the ghastly hoist and stands again. A triumph. Never give up. Well, not just yet.

JESUS

On Palm Sunday American Cousin went to IKEA, assuming that the store would be empty because the English would be in church. Normally I would have thought her raving mad, but as Jesus is all the rage at present, what with everyone flocking to see him tortured on wide screen and this being Easter, peak holy week, perhaps Cousin's assumption was reasonable.

Soon she was stuck in her minicab in a three-lane jam on the North Circular. There must be a terrible accident ahead,' said Cousin to the driver.

No,' said he. 'They're all going to IKEA.'

Panic stations. Cousin felt a sharp pain in her chest and shortness of breath, but there was no turning back. She had to plunge on into the hell of a shopping city, which is where the English now worship. Although I am a second-generation immigrant, I understand their feelings. On Friday nights, I light candles for my mother, then off I go to the supermarket, I enter its portals, I see the peaceful aisles packed neatly with food and I experience bliss. I shop with abandon, I leave, my wallet empty, and I feel cleansed and purged. What joy.

But poor Rosemary cannot let rip in shopping heaven. She represses her desires, shops minimally and feels guilty, guilty, guilty. And no wonder. You wouldn't find Rosemary's family in IKEA on a Sunday. They would all be in church, saying their prayers. This week the church handed out nails to worshippers, and Rosemary's mother grasped hers and lightly stabbed some American relatives with it, to remind them of the meaning of Easter. How odd England must seem to our American visitors.

Rosemary was not present and escaped a stabbing, but she is a let down to her family, because she has lost her faith, and they have been praying for her like billy-o. Even relatives who have passed away are apparently praying for her soul and looking after it, just in case she should want it back one day.

She won't, but she does still hanker after a soul occasionally, and now knows it weighs twenty-one grams. She even thinks I may have one. I certainly have not. We often have a fairly delicate row about this. I long for a fierce and critical row, but Rosemary couldn't bear it. Religion, after all, is about peace and love. If only.

LOOKING FOR THINGS

The other day someone asked Olivia what she did. 'I look for things,' she said, because that's what she spends most of her life doing. Olivia spent the whole of Saturday looking for £60, which she had stuck down the side of her shoe, which she thought would be more sensible than putting it down somewhere, forgetting where she'd put it, and then having to look for it. She couldn't put it in her purse because she didn't know where her purse was, and didn't have time to find it.

Anyway, the £60 disappeared. It must have fallen out of her shoe. Olivia searched everywhere she thought she'd been with the shoe on and, as she had tidied the front garden, she had to look indoors, outdoors and through all the garden rubbish, but she never found it.

I suspect Olivia has too much on her plate: gruelling job, new grandchild, the house being decorated, the extra shopping in fifty-acre furniture warehouses. When one is exhausted, in demand, overworked and over fifty, things tend to get lost, then we have to look for them in this room, that room, upstairs, downstairs and under all the piles of crapola that have mushroomed, because there isn't the time to tidy them, because we are spending the bulk of our lives looking for things

Poor Fielding once spent thirty-six hours looking for a Van Morrison ticket, which he had placed in a book for safe-keeping. He searched every page of every book he owned, hurled his books about, wrecked his house, found long-lost bills, O-level and birth certificates, but no ticket. Three months too late he found it in a Martin Amis.

Last night I lost a letter, my mother's TV guide, the cello rosin, my reading glasses and my mind, because there is only so much searching, grovelling and screaming one can do before one is hot and faint with fatigue and rage and ready to crack up.

'This is why retired people live in bungalows,' says Rosemary. But even in her flat she is still forever losing her purse, keys and phone numbers on bits of paper. This week, *chez nous*, we lost the peeler, strainer, bottle opener, Daughter's glasses, keys, cash card and passport. But at least I found last night's letter. It was stuck under the dinner tray, hiding. With what remained of my mind.

JUST SAY NO

What a struggle Mavis is having with herself. Should she do what she thinks she ought to do but doesn't want to do, or should she just do as she pleases? Last night she spent her whole evening trudging around town with a distant Christian Fundamentalist Republican American relative, when she was desperate to stay indoors resting her aching legs. Why did she not just say no?

Because everybody else had managed to say 'no' already. So Muggins Mavis had to say 'yes'. How could she not? She was the only person left available to entertain the poor visiting relative, whose mother had been very kind to Mavis's mother all those years ago in Texas.

'You had a choice,' said Mavis's brother grandly. How she longed to give him a kicking. What choice? Look after this lonely visitor who everyone else has shunned, or leave her all by herself in a strange city, which was crammed with her relatives, all of whom had said no, probably because they knew it was a fair bet that Mavis or her daughter would say yes.

There is always somebody in a family who will say yes. I hate to generalise, but this person is not often a chap. Do chaps find it easier to say no? I suspect yes. Last week I was rushing about in a sweat and panic chauffeuring, collecting, entertaining and meeting people for various desperate reasons, intensified because the tube trains had gone to hell and the dog was vomiting and limping. Just as I was wondering how I might ever manage to squeeze in a smidgin of work, Gardener suggested that I just say no.

He can say no with ease. Only last week Gardener said no to numerous requests because for two nights running he had reclined on a hammock on the roof, dozing or observing the stars, comets and the beauty of the night sky, which made him feel fatigued during the day, which meant he must rest. All around him our little world was going barmy, but why spring up and function? If one is tired, one won't be much use anyway, reasons Gardener, so have a kip, wake refreshed, then you will be able to help like mad.

Then, with any luck, everything will have been done already by the other persons who have been unable to rest, because they couldn't just say no.

MEASLY ALLOWANCE

A few months ago my mother received some thrilling news. She was entitled to more money. Now that she can barely function and needs care day and night, she may claim higher rate attendance allowance. Fabulous. This made her feel like a wage earner rather than nuisance, and if this entitlement is backdated to her stroke, two years ago, when we ought to have claimed it but didn't realise, we will be living it up.

Then a crushing blow. We may have this measly increment of £20 extra a week, but only backdated for one month, even with medical evidence that we truly deserved it for much longer. But how were we meant to know? It is advertised, says the allowance lady. Where? In libraries. To which the sick, disabled and bedridden may go and read all about it.

But at least we have this paltry allowance. Or do we? The new post office book arrives — no increase. I ring the disability and carers' service for half an hour. Mozart. 'All our operators are busy.' Little-known plodding baroque concerto. At last an answer. 'What is your name? DoB? Address? Number? Problem? Sorry, wrong department. We only make the decisions. We don't distribute the money. We tell the pension service to do that.' I must ring them and complain.

I ring the pension department. Vivaldi. 'All our operators are busy.' Boccherini. I sit clutching my phone, wasting my life, screaming, waiting for news of our pittance. An operator speaks at last. 'Name? DoB? Number? Address? Problem?' Boccherini. They have received no instruction regarding our allowance. Now what? They can't send our money until they're told to. They must await instructions, then they'll recall our book, then they'll send another with the increase added.

When will that be? Who knows? Weeks? Months? In the next life? This is all a monster disappointment to my mother. She has waited eagerly for months for this stingy-mingy little bonus and now her hopes have been dashed. There are only so many dashed hopes that one can tolerate at 97¾.

I relate this dismal tale to Fielding, who remembers Miss Flite – a peripheral spinster figure from *Bleak House*, who kept parrots and hung around the Inns of Court for years waiting for some money that was due to her. She called her parrots Hope and Charity and she died in the gutter. Still waiting.

ABSENT DAUGHTER

Daughter has floated off on yet another exotic holiday, thousands of miles away from her grandma, the Anxiety Queen. My mother wept on and off for twenty-four hours after the beloved granddaughter's departure. The usual terrors rear up: plane crash, drug pedlars, incarceration in foreign gaol, white slave traders, kidnappers or any old accident. You think of it – my mother thought of it first. And now a monster new worry – what if the Grim Reaper snatches my mother before the daughter returns? She is ninety-eight in June. Will she ever see her darling girl again?

My mother lies in bed, white-faced, eyes staring, imagination swirling. Soon her bowels are in uproar. We are desperate for distraction. Even though I am a raving atheist, I say my prayers. Oh, please God, send us a triple bill of *Cagney and Lacey*.

But even my mother has not guessed what the big problem would be. Four days into her hols, Daughter is on the blower at 1 a.m. She is in a fix. Not only did the twitchy Americans stop and search her and the two chums as they changed planes in the USA, interrogated them and lost their luggage, but now, horrors, Daughter's bank has blocked access to her account, just when she is thousands of miles away from her mummy.

How can one ever relax when one has a daughter? We live the drama. I dare not tell my mother about the wretched bank. The bowels will erupt. I ring the emergency bank number in the dead of night. What are they playing at? I have promised Daughter that I will find out.

A foolish promise. The bank will only reveal information to Daughter. She must ring them herself – from Cuba with no money. At last, because I beg them nicely and cry, the bank rings Daughter.

They ring me back.

'I have spoken to your daughter,' a kind lady reports. Praise this woman. She has news of my distant child. 'Is she well? Does she have her money?' I am desperate for news.

'I cannot tell you that.' Nor can the next bank-Johnnie who rings, nor the next, but he can ask me to please run upstairs, find her pin number and e-mail it to her. Can it be that simple? Are the dramas over? Will Daughter make it back for Grandma's birthday? Watch this space.

A BIRTHDAY TOO FAR

Last week my mother was ninety-eight. She was not pleased. I was seated by her bedside trying to convince her that life was fun, fun, fun, when American Cousin rang up, asking what my mother would like for a present.

'To be dead!' she shouted, in the usual way.

I relayed the message.

'What is her second choice?' asked Cousin sensibly. We decided on Turkish delight, because of the eating problems, and a calming, heat-up lavender pad for the misery, fury and terror that are plaguing my mother, now that the ghastly birthday has arrived to remind her of what is going on. And on and on and on.

Who would be ninety-eight? Not my mother. She is forever warning us off it. 'Don't get old,' she instructs all comers, and what a chilling warning she provides: the body gradually failing and mouldering, no outings, no friends left, no proper chatting, no taste and no teeth, which is particularly grim when one is passing a mirror. People ask her how she is: friends, neighbours, nurses, home-care ladies, social workers, doctors and the answer is always the same.

'I want to die!'

Most people tend to go for the robust and upbeat response. 'I'm afraid we can't help you with that one,' says the doctor. 'You've bounced back again.'

'Bye, bye!' my mother waves at the consultant. 'Time for me to go!'

'Not yet!' says the consultant cheerily. 'You're doing ever so well.'

'Bollocks,' snaps my mother. 'I want to die.' She's been begging us to finish her off for months but no one will oblige, then at last her wish nearly came true. Last week we pulled her wraparound cape from the airing cupboard in her room and found it dotted with burns. Horrors! It had been nestling on the immersion heater and secretly smouldering away. The house, dog and whole family could have all gone up in smoke.

My mother was in a fury. 'I could have been killed!' she croaked, outraged, and who can blame her? Why leave the stage when you are not absolutely sure that you are quite ready? You never know, something pleasant may yet happen.

And it does. Daughter staggers home with a clever present – a new television and selection of DVDs. My mother can lie about, surrounded by summer flowers, being pampered, watching films and eating ice-cream. Could be worse.

DOG SHOW

Last month I took the dog and my mother to a dog show. Neither of them liked it. Small dogs yapped for ever, children bounced and bounced their balls and ran about screeching, the sun beat down, the dog begged for water.

I stuck my mother in front of the dogs' agility display in her wheelchair and entered my heavenly dog for several competitions. But events were delayed, nothing much happened, my mother admired a pug, so we gave up and went home. I thought it a charming, mellow event, but my mother did not. 'Too many bloody dogs,' said she, rather ungraciously.

She was reflecting a general mood of dog-hatred which is welling up around here. One small and innocent dog barked at a child and is banned from the park. Another pounced at the park-keeper's rake and must be muzzled for ever, and now false rumours about my own darling dog are circulating and terrifying the neighbourhood.

Meanwhile Fielding has worked himself into a crazed, anti-dog fury. Why? Because his elderly cat was lying in its favourite patch in the front garden waiting to die, when in roared two pitbulls trying to speed things up a bit.

'I'd like to shoot your dogs through the brains,' screamed Fielding harshly, 'if they have any.' But the dog owners were unrepentant, possibly because pussy was unscathed, although the dogs were spouting blood and almost blinded by her vicious claws.

I hardly dare tell Fielding my latest true dog story. I was in the park, with a chum and dogs, when along came this woman with a huge, sausagey dog on a lead. It is always restrained – a tragic sight. But suddenly it experienced a brief moment of bliss. It managed to sniff our dogs' bottoms. At once the woman wrenched it away, as if from rat poison. 'Get off!' she screamed. 'If my dog has impure thoughts he'll go to Hell!'

What a pity that some dog owners are raving mad. They encourage the ghastly anti-dog brigade, which is not what I need, because in eight weeks we are to have another doggie. Only Daughter, Gardener and I are thrilled. Scarcely anyone else approves. They are fairly certain that my dog will eat the dinky new puppy for breakfast, or teach it to be a killer.

No chance. Just chill out, you critics. Or my dogs will bite your ear off.

THE END?

I was driving along in my car wailing because I thought my mother had had it. I could barely get her to swallow a morsel of food. She has rejected Complan, Ensure and water – the last-resort snacks. What is one to do with a failing and depressed mother? I personally am shit-scared of death. Perhaps my mother is also panicking and needs help.

I call the rabbi. Could he please visit? Yes, says he, but I must ask her first. He won't mind if she says no. He can take rejection. But what will my mother do if I start droning about rabbis? What if I blub? Will she think the Reaper is just behind me?

No. She perks up at once at the magic word rabbi, applies her lip-stick, does her hair, sits up straight and returns to life. The rabbi arrives, looking rather dashing in a dark-blue suit and swizzy tie. I expected some muted last whisperings, but no. They chatter about Tate Modern, holidays in Eastern Europe, our family photographs. This is clearly not a Last Visit.

There is nothing like visitors and aggravation to perk up a half-starved and dismal mother. We have loads of both crammed into one week: hairdresser, doctors, friends, Cousin from Barrow and police all visit. Parking wardens give my mother's carer two penalty charges for nothing (they were Inexperienced), robbers smash the car window and steal our disabled card.

Can we keep up this stimulating flood of events? It works a treat. Soon my mother is eating chops. One of life's mysteries. How can she eat lamb chops if she cannot eat soft bits of pear, carefully peeled by me? How I sometimes long to throw the bits of pear in the air and scream, but I eat it myself instead. And one good thing about my mother's meagre diet. She is certainly not obese. We have made up a little poem:

'Want to lose weight?
Be ninety-eight!'

We feel that when things are grisly, we may as well have a laugh. But sadly I dare not read all this piece to my mother. If one thing frightens her more than the Reaper, it is me revealing our ethnic roots. She is still sure that the Nazis will be round, hurling bricks through the windows. That would be a little too stimulating. Even for us.

FEEDING

What fun is life when one does not even fancy the tiniest snack? I am plying my mother with every known delicacy, but she rejects them all, pulling ghastly faces, throwing up or chewing at the odd mouthful as if it were strychnine. How difficult it is to maintain a sunny mood when one is the cook in these circumstances.

'Make some soups,' says Rosemary bossily. 'That's what we did for Auntie. Make some rice pudding.'

I make them. Four teaspoons of soup go down, one of rice pudding. I try mango and banana smoothie. It tastes like heaven. Who could possibly reject such a delicious drinkie? My mother can. She tastes it and expresses revulsion. To her it is rat poison. Quick. The sick bowl. We try Complan. Erk. And Ensure. Erk. Every known variety of soup. Erk. Fruit purees, soft fruit – peeled, cut up, squashed. Yuk. Patés, soft cheeses, soft puddings. Yuk, yuk and yuk again. We are down to two barely acceptable options: lamb chops and smoked salmon – one tiny morsel at a time.

What is going on? Are the bucketfuls of medication my mother must swallow daily affecting the taste buds? Is it the false teeth? No, because the dentist has checked them and they are a perfect fit. So it must be the nearly one hundred-year-old digestive system packing in.

Then round come the district nurses. 'Do you have leg ulcers?' they ask my mother. No. Wrong person. Somewhere out there is another Hanson with at least one ghastly complaint that my mother does not have. A reason to be cheerful. But as the nurses are here anyway they have a look. My mother has mouth thrush. Scrub the tongue with a brush, rinse with this and that mouthwash, smarm this here, dab that there, watch another bit of the body mouldering away, go slowly raving mad, have a little cry out of sight.

Every bit of my poor mother is giving up the ghost, except her. She is still as strong as several oxen. I blame her healthy lifestyle: no smoking, no drugs, hardly any drinking, just the odd Martini and lemonade, only homemade food, lots of dancing, living mainly by the seaside and not a single mouthful of Mcdonald's in her whole life. That is the way to be nearly a hundred. If that's what you really want.

GRANDMA CLARICE BY AMY

Sometimes my daughter takes over the feeding and the writing.

'Can you make the lunch?' my mother asks.

'Why can't *you*?' I want to know. 'I'm trying to work!'

'I'm *also* trying to work but Grandma has crapped herself and I'm cleaning her up. What would you rather do? The choice is yours – clean up crap or make lunch?'

I make lunch.

Mum doesn't want to eat because she has been cleaning up crap. Grandma doesn't want to eat because she's upset that she crapped herself. I don't want to eat because I can smell disinfectant and everyone is talking about crap.

We put Grandma back into bed all clean. The TV is on loudly. We both go back to working on our computers. Grandma does nothing. She stares at the TV. Crapping herself must have been the most exciting part of her day.

I go into her room and sit on the end of the bed.

'How you feeling? I ask.

'Ufol,' she replies in a slurred voice.

I start to recount a story, about trying to buy a football top for my boyfriend; she smiles. Her eyes are watery and glazed, like an old pug's.

'Is she going to die? Is this it?' I ask my mother in the kitchen, after the crapping and cleaning and cooking saga, which happens in a slightly different way every day.

'I don't know. When she moved in I thought she'd last a week, a year at the most.'

My grandmother, my mother's mother, moved in with us over a

decade ago, when she was eighty-eight. At first this was good. She was funny, bossy, animated, emotional, loud, cross. Then two years ago she had a stroke. Now she is quiet and sad and waiting to die. My mother and I are waiting too. We know that she is waiting and she knows that we are waiting. You could call it a waiting game but there is nothing fun or game-like about it. The only game it makes me think of is a really long and drawn-out game of Monopoly when you've had to mortgage everything, you're in jail, you've got no money, the person next to you has Mayfair and you just want it to be over.

Before the stroke my mother didn't like to leave her alone in the house much, *in case something happened.* On the one night she did go out – something happened.

I'm sitting upstairs in my room. We've had dinner together and Grandma has been talking about her friends cheating at bridge. Then she told me a story she tells on a regular basis about Grandpa and how she met him at a dance, where she had been wearing a backless dress. She 'sensed' him watching her, turned around and they fell in love, but really, she felt, it was the dress that did it.

For some reason I feel like I should really go and talk to her again, before bed. I don't know why, I don't have anything to say, I know she'll bend my ear with the same old stories but I go anyway. Maybe I sense that this could be my last chance.

As I walk into her room she immediately starts talking from where she left off earlier. 'And then I saw the old bugger looking at Cynthia's cards. Well, I think, I'm not having that, I gave Cynthia a kick under the table and then I said to Martha, I said, "Your husband's a bloody cheat!" Ooh, I tell you, she didn't like that, couldn't believe it, but I saw it! "He's not," she says. "I'm not," he says, but I know what I saw and so I just got up and I said to Cynthia, "You can stay but I'll be damned if I'm having my game of bridge ruined by a pair of bloody cheats." Oooh, you should have seen their faces . . . '

'Are you watching this?' I ask, pointing at the telly.

'No, don't turn over. I'm waiting for Graham Norton, oooh he's so funny! So rude! Always talking about willies! Did you see it last week when . . . ?'

'Grandma!'

I look at her and she is staring in a vacant way in the direction of the telly.

'Grandma?'

One side of her face looks funny. It's all droopy and there is a tear rolling down the other side.

'Grandma! Grandma!'

She doesn't blink. The corner of the left side of her mouth is right down her chin, her cheek sagging, her left eye lower than her right. When I wave my hand across her face, she does not react. I shake her gently by the shoulder. She flops to the side.

'Grandma, are you all right?'

She does not move.

'Grandma, please say something.'

Tears start to fall down my cheeks. Tears of fear – fear of something that has happened, fear of something that can't be stopped, tears that fall fast. I'm not making a noise. This is not the sort of crying when you have noise and snot and tears, just the tears on their own. Tears that know they don't need to be concealed because the person they are for does not know what is going on. She is still. She has stopped. That is why her face has flopped I do not know why I am crying, but something in me realises before I do that this is Grandma dying.

I watch in fast-forward through rain as the ambulance men come. They are frightened of the dog. They put Grandma on a stretcher and cover her with a red blanket. I remember my mum saying, 'If anything happens, don't take her to the Whittington Hospital.

They take her to the Whittington Hospital.

I sit with her on a stretcher in a corridor for hours. Nobody looks at her. Nobody rushes her anywhere. No handsome doctor comes and says not to worry, she'll be all right. We just wait in the corridor.

'What's your name?' says a patronising nurse.

'Clarice,' I say. 'She can't say her name, look at her!'

'Ahh,' says the nurse.

'She can't say her name because she's had a bloody stroke!' My voice starts to rise and become shrill.

'How long has she been like this?'

'Just tonight, she has just had *a stroke*. Where is the fucking doctor?'

'Please don't swear.'

One nurse goes, another comes and goes, and they all ask the same questions and every time I try to explain that this is not my grandma, that my grandma is very different from this normally, that this is very bad, that she is normally very talkative, that this is an emergency. They look at me as if I'm mad, that I'm deluded, that this is an old dying lady and I can't accept it.

'How old did you say she is?' asks another nurse.

'Ninety-six.'

'Ahh,' she says in a 'that explains it' kind of voice.

'But she is not usually like this, I know she's old but seriously she's usually very, you know, awake!'

The nurse puts her head on one side and smiles at me sympathetically. She does not believe me. I want to slap her, but instead I say, 'Where is the doctor?'

'He'll be round soon, lots of emergencies tonight.'

'This *is* an emergency!'

She smiles and walks away.

After four hours a twelve-year-old looking doctor arrives and I tell him what is wrong with her Why did I let them bring her to the Whittington? I think. I start to cry and then to my great relief my mum arrives.

My grandma spends the next two days on a ward where no one seems to do anything. My mother and I take it in turns to visit every couple of hours. We find her waiting in her own wee, waiting in her own shit, falling out of the bed, unable to sit up. This is not the place for her to recover. This is a place where nurses with fat arses walk up and down kissing their teeth at old women and showing them no respect or love. This is the Whittington Hospital and it is a joke.

For these first couple of days she cannot talk at all, she can only sign or point at things she wants. I make her a sign on a piece of cardboard that says I NEED TO GO TO THE TOILET PLEASE, which she can hold up as the nurses idle by.

'She won't be able to talk again,' says one doctor.

'She may be able to talk again,' says another.

'She will probably be able to say a few words,' says a third. 'But at her age she probably won't live long enough to regain her vocabulary in time.'

'Balls,' says Grandma after two days. It's a miracle. We jump up and down and hug her, we are so proud.

'Say it again,' says my mother.

'Balls,' says Grandma smiling.

'Again,' I say.

'Balls,' she says loudly. My mother and I are thrilled and tell everyone who asks after her the amazing news: 'Grandma said Balls!'

When it is time to leave the ward of uncaring nurses and kleptomaniac patients, one of whom keeps stealing Grandma's slippers, she stands up ready to go and as we get to the door she turns round to the ward and the nurses, raises two fingers and says, 'Balls to ya all,' and if that is not enough, she follows this with what is undeniably the word 'Bollocks'. We clap and cheer and laugh all the way home. 'Balls to you all . . . bollocks,' we chant and she joins in.

A week passes and Grandma can say shit and crap too. We get her to repeat all the swear words as often as possible and then we try to teach her names. We print out a piece of paper with the names of family and friends on it in large letters. My mother Michele becomes Misle, I become Illy instead of Amy, as does my dog, whose name is Lily. Hazel, my best friend is Izle: though she can say 'Hay' and 'Zel' separately, she cannot put them together. She cannot say Gardener, my mum's boyfriend. But one day as we are practising words, she tries to tell me something. She's in a bit of a bate – someone has annoyed her.

'Who are you talking about?' I ask.

'Imma.'

'Who?'

'IMMA.'

'I don't know who that is, can you point to the name?'

She bashes her finger into the word 'Gardener'.

'Gardener? Are you cross with Gardener?' I ask.

'Yes,' she replies. 'Parasite.'

'Parasite?'

'Parasite,' she repeats.

'Wonderful!' I cry. 'Say it again'

Then I call up the stairs to Mum, 'Something wonderful has happened! Grandma called Gardener a parasite!'

'Wonderful!' my mother replies.

The GP says that all this swearing is quite normal. Swear words are the easiest to say after a stroke. Names are difficult because they only stand for one thing, a person. We sit with her for hours asking her to repeat words, breaking them into syllables. But it's not single words she wants to say. She wants to talk, non-stop. Some things come out quite clearly and other things make no sense. Yes and no are frequently confused as is shaking and nodding her head. We listen hard. Every exchange of words becomes a game of charades. She looks exasperated when she can't say what she wants. Sometimes she just says complete nonsense and if she realises I don't know what she's saying, she gives up and shouts 'Balls'.

I am looking after Grandma this evening.

'What would you like for dinner?'

Grandma shrugs her shoulders and looks depressed.

'Chops?' I say cheerfully, knowing she likes them.

She nods.

'With which vegetables?' I continue in my most cheery singsong voice.

She shrugs her shoulder.

'Broccoli?'

Shrug.

'Mashed potatoes!'

Nod.

'Courgettes?'

Shrug.

'What then?'

She moves her finger up and down.

'A long vegetable?'

She nods.

'Leeks?'

She shakes her head.

'Celery?'

She shakes her head and says, 'White.'

'It's a white vegetable!' I cry as if she has given me the password to a safe full of gold.

She nods and smiles.

'Cabbage?'

She shakes her head.

'Definitely *not* leeks?'

She shakes her head.

'Swede?'

She shakes her head.

'Can you draw the mystery vegetable?'

She nods. I give her a pencil and the back of a bank statement to draw on. She starts reading the statement.

'Draw the vegetable.' I point at the plain side of the paper. She looks at the plain paper blankly, turns it round and starts to read the numbers on the statement. I turn the paper round, replace the pencil in her fingers at a better angle and give her a book to lean on.

'Can you draw the white vegetable?'

'Yes,' she says and nods. Then she turns the paper over and reads the bank statement again.

I turn it around again, touch the hand clasping the pencil and point at the paper.

'Draw the vegetable,' I say in my most enthusiastic voice.

She draws a parsnip. The parsnip is perfectly in proportion and very neat. This morning she could not hold her spoon at breakfast. She can barely write anything. Every number she says is zero or seven. When she says phone numbers she says zero or seven in a different voice eleven times to make a phone number. But she has drawn a perfect parsnip on the back of Barclays bank statement.

'Parsnip!' I shriek. She smiles, I am so pleased and it took only fifteen minutes!

Over the last two years she has learnt more words. But these days she hardly gets out of bed. She's too tired even to try and speak.

It's late and I'm working. I make a coffee.

'Got a biscuit?' I ask Mum.

'Grandma's room,' she calls up the stairs.

When I move back home the three generations of women in our family all live in the same house on separate floors. Grandma is on the first floor with a Stannah stairlift from the ground floor to her room, strategically placed next to the bathroom. The middle floor is my mother's room and the top floor is where I hide/dwell.

I pass my mother's room, down the next flight, past the bathroom. The walls of the corridor here are cramped with outsized oil paintings of bouquets of flowers and bowls of fruit that my grandmother painted when she could hold a brush. We call this corridor 'The Gallery'.

Sitting half up in bed, her mouth open, her eyes closed, her skin more grey than I've seen it before, is Grandma. The only way I can think to describe the way she looks is dead. I take one step into the room. On my right is a small dresser with the box of biscuits on it. Across the far wall is her bed, under the window, which looks out on to the back garden. Her head is in the right-hand corner opposite the dresser. I reach into the box and take a biscuit. Quietly. I take a step back from the dresser. She is dead, I think. I take another step back, I'm now in the doorway. She's dead. I'm going to leave this room with this chocolate biscuit and let my mum find her. Mum will be up in five minutes. If Grandma's dead it makes no difference, except I don't want to be the one to discover her. No sooner have I thought this than I take a step forward. I can't take a chocolate biscuit from my dead grandma, I think. I can't believe that my first reaction was to leave her. What is wrong with me? I go over to the bed and put my face close to her. A faint breath from her lips touches my cheek and I leave the room, with a great sense of relief and a biscuit.

Grandma's full name is Clarice Queenie Hanson and she used to talk, a lot. She is the most talkative person I have ever met, in fact, but now she can barely talk at all.

Her parents were Jews who came to England from Latvia. They were middle class and arranged a marriage for her to an older, rich man with epilepsy. At eighteen the fits frightened her and when he wasn't ill she didn't like him. At twenty-two she ran away and met my grandpa. He was a poor Jew from Camden Town with seven siblings and together they eloped to Ruislip.

When she could talk she told me that she drove a motorbike, that she was the first woman in Manchester to wear trousers, that she owned a cake shop when she was in her twenties, that her family were the first in the street to have a bath, that she loved to dance, that she had a brother called Cyril and a sister called Cissy and she loved Cyril and hated Cissy and that she was much prettier than her sister.

She was the oldest and used to babysit her younger brother and sister just as I babysit her now.

My grandma was, at one point in my life, the person I loved more than any other living thing on earth. I loved her more than my mother, father, grandfather and siblings. I loved to cuddle her, to smell her, to sit with her, talk to her, cook with her, walk with her, I loved to be close to her. She would spend hours playing with me in the garden, making me fairy costumes and flower garlands out of convolvulus. She once made me a pinafore of purple fabric, with eight pockets, one for each of my guinea pigs, with their names embroidered in pink on to each pocket. Dressing up was an important part of our relationship. We would be different characters and she would bring stories to life. It wasn't one-sided either, she too would dress up. I remember her doing the dance of the seven veils in the living room of her flat in Hove to attract the attention of my grandpa who had his hearing aid turned off and his sight tuned in to the horse racing on television. Both of us wore eight layers and then danced around flinging different coloured fabrics at my grandpa's bald head.

Now she is the baby, I am in another room from her. Actually I am in the room which is furthest away from hers.

I am late for work this morning and even though she can't say my name properly any more, I know that's what she's saying as I close the door. I return in the late afternoon feeling guilty. I am tired because I've been busy but I know the day has been longer for her. All she has done is lie in her bed watching the birds out of her window through little binoculars. It's lonely in her bed with only the birds to look at. And company is the one thing I can give her, though I find it hard to give it to her all the time and that's what makes me feel guilty.

'I'm home,' I call up the stairs cheerfully. 'Up in a minute,' and go down the stairs to the kitchen. I get out her special flowery tray and place her matching teacups with saucers on it. Then a little plate with cheese on crackers and biscuits, arranged in the shape of a flower, knowing she'll like it and lessening my guilt.

I take up the tray and she smiles and slurs what is probably, 'How was your day?' I spread a towel under the tray on her lap and a napkin round her neck. She tries to eat the crackers but I look round and the cheese is mixed with spit and dribbling down her chin, the cracker is sticking out of her mouth at a strange angle, at which point I realise that her false teeth have come out and I have to turn away. Watching her is making me feel sick. I feel angry that it makes me feel sick and guilty all over again. I wipe her chin and pop her teeth back in but concentrate on the telly.

'Stop talking till you've eaten it,' I say as the teeth came out again and the cheese drops everywhere and bits of cracker spill all over the bed. She looks down, sad, embarrassed. I feel horrible and look away. I start to write in my diary. I can't eat because every mouthful I take reminds me of what is chewed up and falling from hers.

'Ya've gat larvely andwritirg,' she whispers sounding like a drunk. 'Better van ya mammy's.' She can't read it; she can just see the shape of the words.

Behind her glazed eyes I think I can see pride. I feel like a bitch.

'All the boys liked me the best!' Grandma used to exclaim. 'More than Cissy, I was their favourite, she was jealous rotten when I married Daddy.'

Grandma is not keen on many men and has been known to behave like a battle-axe. However there have been men who made her blush. A dashing Irish friend of mine, for instance who used to kiss her hand when he dropped round after college. *He* never got *his* ciggies confiscated. And anyone else who complimented her appearance or cooking made this strong, witty, loud old lady seem to turn to jelly.

As I say goodbye to her today, the sun is shining through her window.

'Would you like some sunglasses?' I ask. She nods and I fetch her some comedy Elvis glasses I have from a party. I put the enormous gold Elvis glasses over my grandma's old watery eyes on her wrinkly face and she smiles. Then I take a photo of her with my phone.

'Ohh, oooh,' she says pointing at the phone and turning it around.

'It's got a camera on it,' I explain.

'Oooohhh,' she says in amazement.

I turn the phone round so she can see herself as a ninety-eight-year-old Elvis and we both laugh.

'Sam wore these at the party,' I explain, 'with a football top, a wig and a moustache!'

'Lord!' she exclaims.

I lean down to kiss her goodbye.

'Ya luk im?' she asks.

'I do like him.'

'I wanna shee im.'

'You want to meet him?'

She nods.

'Well, next time he's round, I'll bring him up to say hello, OK? You can meet him.'

She nods her head and smiles.

That day she has her hair done. She wants her hair looking nice and a new nightie on because she has a new, young, Australian carer called Wes who is very 'amshom' and wears beads and jeans, she tells me, smiling and going pink.

The following evening I have a girly night with my friends and we are sitting upstairs drinking pink wine, watching *Sex And the City* and gorging ourselves on Milk Tray, when my mother comes up.

'Grandma's trying to tell me something and I don't know what she's talking about,' she says. 'She thinks she's meeting Sam tonight, she won't go to bed or put her hairnet on until she's seen him with her hair done. Did you tell her he was coming to meet her?'

'I did, but he's not coming till tomorrow.'

'What a relief, I thought she'd lost it.'

I go downstairs and explain that she isn't going to meet him tonight.

'But would you like the girls to see your hair?' I ask.

'Naaa, no bova,' she puts her navy hairnet on over her newly set white hair and goes to sleep.

The next night I go out with Sam and get drunk. We tumble in around midnight. That's odd, I think, the house is in darkness apart from a light coming from Grandma's room.

'Oh no, she's waited up to meet you!'

'Meet me?'

'I promised she could see you today.'

'Now?'

'Now!'

I run up the stairs and find her sitting upright in bed dozing.

'Are you awake?' I whisper.

She nods.

'Were you waiting up to meet him?' I ask.

She nods.

'Well, he's downstairs, are you not too tired?' She shakes her head.

I lift her up into a better position, a receiving-visitors-position, and we remove her hairnet to reveal her still very neat white hair.

'Come in,' I call and Sam comes in.

She smiles and instantly goes pink.

He says everything right – 'Hello, lovely to meet you!' He shakes her hand. 'Your hair looks nice. Are you feeling all right?' She nods and smiles.

'Yesh, ank oo. Hello.'

'So lovely to meet you properly. I met you before but very briefly, on my way upstairs, but it's good to meet you in person!'

She gazes up at him and then looks at me and then at him.

'She's good,' she says.

'I know,' he replies. 'I think so.'

She smiles and says, 'Good nat.'

'Good night.'

'Good night, Grandma.'

'Fank oo,' she whispers as I lean down to kiss her forehead.

I think of her all alone in the dark, waiting, waiting to meet my boyfriend, keeping her hair nice, remembering, for two days, while I forgot and whizzed about being twenty-five.

'She's got all her marbles,' says Sam. 'My grandma's much worse and she's not that old.'

It's hard to remember what she was. It is hard for people to meet her now and have any idea of the person she was inside this old body. But, unlike the nurses, Sam saw her, just a glimmer, a spark of Clarice Queenie, my grandma. That is the grandma I will always try to remember.

I didn't know whether to laugh or cry as I passed her room today. Through the gap in the door I saw this old lady, sitting on the commode, big white knickers drooping round her knees, staring blankly at the wall. She cannot read any more so the mobile library brings her these story tapes. I can hear one now. It interrupts my sad thoughts. The whole house can hear it. A middle-aged female narrator booming from Grandma's stereo.

"'*It's sort of like that. Wow, I'm dizzy,*' Nell said, breathless now. '*I felt a tingling inside, not unpleasant. Almost like you do when you're thinking — really thinking — about sex.*'"

And I'd thought she was sitting there thinking about death.

DIVORCE

Gardener and I are to separate. I was going to keep it a secret, but Gardener told his friend on the phone. 'We've given up,' said he cheerily, 'because of mutual hatred.' What a relief. Now we can speak freely about all the ghastly little things that make one want to scream and kick the wardrobe.

Life was much better when we had our own establishments. Then we could put on our clean clothes and best manners, go visiting each other and be charming. That way we never noticed all those odd little habits that are bound to annoy when one must endure them day and night, for ever: Gardener's mad computer fractalling, detritus collections and arrangements, strange feeding habits and sleeping patterns, love of raving, glaring light and loud African pirate radio. My dog-kissing, resentful mother and daughter, poor kitchen hygiene and penchant for gloom and Purcell. What a hopeless combination.

And what about Gardener's marijuana binges, followed by massive consumption of chocs, ice-cream and jumbo extra helpings of cake? Naturally my mother thought him a greedy porker. How was I to explain? 'No, Mummy. It's all right. It's not greed, it's drugs.'

'I think everybody should live separately,' says Fielding, dreaming of the heavenly things he could do, if only his wife and two daughters were not present: wallow in two-hour baths, play screaming rock and roll, watch non-stop footer, cut his toenails and leave the trimmings about. Perhaps he is sensible to remain under strict supervision, because nasty habits tend to intensify with age, especially if one is faintly weird to start with.

I notice Gardener is tending more towards the hippie life, finding new chums in health-food shops, at Stonehenge and among the

Celtic fringe. Treehouses and road protests have been mentioned. 'I'm up for that,' said Gardener, with the faraway look that I have learnt to dread. And once Gardener was on the sofa, I allowed both dogs on the bed. A dangerous move.

I think I see the future. Daughter will leave home, my mother will be confined to her garret, Gardener will be eating strange mushrooms, droning and being artistic in a tree-top commune and I will be a gabbling, raggedy dog-woman, tottering across the Heath, then coming home to my bleak, empty and silent new dwelling to tinkle away at the harpsichord. It is never too late to have fun.

UPS AND DOWNS

For months my mother seems to have been fading away, scarcely eating a crumb, the Reaper breathing down her neck, but since the new puppy has arrived she has perked up enormously. We now have two dogs. I suspect anxiety had been making her poorly. Being an imaginative woman, forced to idle in bed, she had dredged up a great swirl of frightful thoughts: that she would be neglected, left alone stinking and starving in her garret, commode filling, bedclothes reeking and sodden, while we were all entranced and diddling with the new dog downstairs. Or worse still, we wouldn't even get it home, because we'd crash the car collecting it from Bournemouth, and her daughter, granddaughter and baby dog would all die in one go.

Then what? Hell beckoned my mother, towards a slow and wretched death in an institution, abused by poorly paid, cruel and heartless staff. See how her anxieties spread like galloping impetigo, once they get going.

Luckily, none of this happens. No one crashes or dies, she is not neglected. Even the puppy visits her. She gazes at it, her heart melts, she eats whole meals, things are looking up. But never rejoice too soon, I say. When everything is going swimmingly, you can bet your life something grisly is bound to happen.

Round comes the builder to look at our ceiling. Some cracks have suddenly begun to grow and gape. Builder goes pale. The ten-ton ceiling rose is apparently hanging by one screw, ready to crush me and the dogs to death as we cluster beneath it day and night. Back comes the builder at dawn the next day to tear down half the ceiling. Imagine the filth and chaos. And that very same night our new puppy begins vomiting and choking.

Off we go to the emergency vet. A squillion-pound bill is estimated, of which I must pay half before leaving the trembling baby there, possibly to be sliced open at midnight. Back home, my mother is pallid and weeping, sinking again. She clutches the doggie's photo to her breast. 'Don't cry for me when I'm dead,' she blubs movingly. But what has that got to do with anything?

Then happy times. The dog only had wind. The ceiling is mended. We are still alive. Visitors and dogs crowd my mother's room. She rises from the nearly-dead. Up we go again. But for how long?

MALE BRAIN

Sylvia has been having a grisly time trying to find a new lawnmower and working out why Beckham was only allowed on to the pitch for ten minutes in that game with Real. Being over eighty, she has few peers who wish to chat about football, all lawnmower shops are an endless drive away into the unknown, and Sylvia hates consulting maps.

No wonder she is having trouble. Football, lawnmowers and maps are in male-brain territory. This is a foreign land to us girls. Research has found (I read it in the newspaper) that frequently female brains are empathic and male brains are systematic. My own research confirms this study. In the park, I spotted some youths at play, ripping off half a tree and thrashing the remaining branches to bits.

They gazed admiringly at the elder of my dogs, with its huge muscles and slathering jaws. 'Does it go fast?' asked one, whacking at the bench with his bicycle chain. Then they laughed mockingly as it pounced gently on its pink, squeaky hedgehog.

But sometimes the male brain is of use. I often call for Gardener's help: lifting furniture, or when the computer cocks up or machinery must be dealt with. Last week I begged him, on my knees, to promise on his life to record a video for me, vital research for my lifetime project. My future depended on this video.

I returned home to find that Gardener had not done as requested. Had he forgotten? No. *He couldn't find the remote control!* What about manual? *He couldn't work out how to do it!*

This is not as odd as it sounds. The female brain does manual – one button says channel, another says record. Easy. But the extreme male brain eschews this method. It soars ahead, up into a rarified world of zapping, remote-control systems and complications, unaware that down here on the ground, divorce is brewing and a girly breakdown taking place.

Fortunately, some chaps have a balanced brain. I ring Fielding, to confirm that he has one. 'Bollocks,' shouts Mrs Fielding from the background, and she is right. 'Empathic or systematic?' muses Fielding. 'You mean ditzy or cerebral,' and then starts droning about footer and Beckham's beauty. 'He's up there with Michaelangelo,' says he in a sickening way. I was going to tell Sylvia to ring him up for a football chat, but why bother?

SHOPPING IN HELL

Shopping is rather like childbirth, I find. You forget the pain and ghastly bits and go and do it all over again. So I went birthday/Christmas shopping with Daughter in town. A big mistake. In all clothes shops catering for younger persons, it is Guantanamo torture music but louder. After two hours I was partially deaf and clinging to the edge of sanity. I sat ashen-faced on some stairs, the brain mashed by thunderous pop-crap. I swear it is worse than ever before. Even Daughter could scarcely bear it.

No wonder we are all growing fat, deaf and barmy. As a qualified music therapist, can I suggest that the hideous battery of noise in public places is damaging our mental health? Music is meant to be good for one. Look what it can do: raise the spirits, calm the soul (for those who think they have one), soothe and unite a maddened crowd of thousands, connect with faraway bits of brain and enhance the quality of bulls' semen.

I experienced none of these qualities while shopping and returned home knackered and deranged, knocked my mother's sweet-sour chicken and rice all over the carpet, flung myself to the ground, screaming 'fuck it' repeatedly and rather crudely, and set my poor mother off wailing and wanting to die again.

Luckily Daughter rushed to our aid, mopped up the carpet and her grandma, remade the bed, banned me from the room and excused me from any further shopping. She will take her birthday money and go with her friend Rae, who can cope with squillion decibel noise, and dances all the way while shopping.

'It's a bit Tennessee Williams in your house,' said Fielding when I told him about the shameful, post-shopping episode. He is right. It's all heat, dogs, mess, screaming, blubbing and seething here, and on top of the usual overheated carry-on, Gardener and I are in emotional turmoil. But there is one terrific advantage to this sort of eruption. Once the boil has burst one can sometimes calm down and spot a solution. I spotted a simple one straightaway: no more shopping for me. No more searching for presents. Everyone can have Palestinian olive oil for Christmas, whether they like it or not.

Meanwhile, I'm walking past the newsagent's and notice a tragic headline on a billboard: 'Killer driven mad by noise'. Shoppers take note.

LIGHTING UP TIME – SAD

I find Gardener in the kitchen crouched over a small radio. It is blaring cacophonous music. I cannot eat my pineapple in a relaxed way. 'What is that vile noise?' I ask.

It's a tune I'm interested in,' says Gardener. How I long to scream 'What tune?' and kick his radio out of the window, but I may not, because Gardener is poorly. He suspects that he has SAD – Seasonal Affective Disorder.

For three days and nights he has been away. Three heavenly days of gloom and quiet for me, but now he is back again, snapping on all the lights, 150 watts everywhere, and to go with the lights, Gardener needs sound – input, input – jangly, diddly youth music, Club Asia and the World Service and the tellies roaring with sport, all at once. And action. Gardener is forever phoning and recording the radio stations, they phone him, he phones chums, who must listen, phone in, phone him back, until he has built a great criss-cross web of phonings – blah blah, blinding glare, jingle jangle.

Meanwhile, downstairs in a darkened corner of the living room behind the sofa, the dogs and I are huddled with our hair on end. My mother knows nothing of this. She is in bed with the telly or audio tapes or both also blaring, and upstairs, Daughter occasionally has a dance, pretending she is clubbing – thumpety-thump-thump.

Sometimes I wake before dawn while they are all asleep and wander about the house in the darkness and silence, being happy. I light a flickering candle, get out a notebook and quill pen and stare out into the silvery garden. I play barely audible tunes on the tinkly harpsichord, muted. Perhaps I am the odd one here.

In the Northern hemisphere, I would be normal. Persons up there carry on normally in the dark, 'They pull themselves together and eat lots of fish,' says Olivia strictly.

Only Olivia understands me, because she too has lived with a SAD person. Her daughter. She even bought the daughter a SAD light. Daughter sat in a white room with the light blazing. There was no improvement to speak of. Olivia was infuriated. 'It was bloody expensive,' says she. And where is it now? 'Left in a squat somewhere.'

So never mind the Festivals of Light. How about a Festival of Dark, especially for me?

XMAS REPRIEVE

Dinnertime in front of the telly in our house and on comes a sparkly advert for Xmas food, starring Jamie Oliver. It enrages my mother, the Christmas Hater. 'Shaarrupp!' she roars, rather ungraciously. This heralds the annual burst of profoundly horrible behaviour. How ever are we going to manage our festivities without stabbing each other?

Then a ray of hope. We have a reprieve. Daughter is invited to spend Christmas with Sam the Boyfriend's family at a much better venue than our house. It has swimming pool with wave machine, giant trampoline and ponies. In Essex. 'Think *Birds of a Feather*,' says he. What more could a girl want? We are all thrilled. No enormous turkey corpse for me, no cooking and sweating about the kitchen, no overindulgence, no nausea. And Daughter will be having fun, which is tricky in our house.

But she hesitates. 'Promise you'll tell me if you're miserable, Mum,' says she, 'and I won't go.' Now that I am almost divorced, she imagines me all alone with her grandma, Madame Scrooge, who bans crackers, extravagant gifts, sparkly trees, or any rejoicing associated with Jesus. There we will sit, dour and isolated, with a sawdust vegeburger for festive lunch. Daughter does not realise that this is my sort of heaven.

'Stop boasting,' shouts Rosemary. How she envies our lonely Christmas. She is having twelve people to lunch, some of a deeply religious persuasion, all wodged into her tiny kitchen. She must make sure she's heating up the gravy during grace. This is a fairly tragic time for her. She has no faith and no grandchildren to fill stockings for, only her own three grown-up children.

She might be pleased to know that my daughter also requires a stocking. She must have it before she goes away. 'Then we can have turkey when I get back. I'll cook it,' says Daughter excitedly, and we'll need crackers, drink and pudding to go with it, and a tree, because she's only away for two days, and are the fairy lights still working? And why don't I go to the favourite supermarket on Christmas Eve, where they'll be throwing turkeys away, then I can buy two, freeze one, and what about cards? And the dogs need new Xmas squeakies, Grandma's clothes are all crap, she needs new ones and some sales are even starting before Christmas . . . Aaargh.

TWO HATS

I notice that Gardener's true character, repressed for twelve years by me, is breaking out now that he has become a more or less homeless nomad. For a start, he is wearing two hats: a woolly one with a black trilby on top, and has been raving at Stonehenge, returning days later, pupils dilated, hats on and too knackered to remove his several tonnes of possessions which are clogging our basement.

I feel a bitter tone creeping into my narrative. Because I was planning New Year home improvements: a sparkly clean kitchen, properly trained dogs, and most of all – an empty basement. But Gardener still has no other storage facility. He can only redistribute in dribs and drabs.

At last he awakes and functions. 'Look at this,' says he excitedly, lugging a gargantuan box into the hall. It is labelled Chaos Box. Inside is a mad swirl of crumpled paper and plastic parcel strapping. Hoorah. It is only rubbish. He can throw it away. Wrong again. It is an art work, to be treasured for ever. No wonder we fell out. Off goes Gardener, hats on, up and down the path with bundles, boxes, art works, stone and twig collections and beloved assorted rubble, carful after carful, en route to elsewhere. A poignant scene.

Then another poignant scene upstairs. I have told my mother that Gardener is leaving, the basement is being cleared, much of the crap still down there is mine and I plan to throw it away. I thought she would rejoice, but no. She panics. Are any of her paintings down there about to be thrown away by mistake? Absolutely not. But this is the Anxiety Queen. She must look and check. Suddenly, in the dead of night, I hear a noise. It is my mother, rearing up on her Zimmer to search the basement.

But within seconds she is toppling sideways – crash goes the vase of flowers, the water, the drink of juice, the false-teeth beaker. I catch my mother and haul her on to the bed. She sits wailing in her nightie, sodden by all the spillage. What sort of a life is this? A divorced daughter, a house full of drek, her paintings lost, it is 2005 and she is still here.

'You'll be getting your birthday card from the Queen,' says an innocent visitor.

'Fuck the Queen!' shouts my mother. Another happy New Year.

MOTHER ON SITE

People often stare at me in an admiring way and say what a saintly person I am to have my ancient mama in residence. Wrong. Having a mother on site is the easy way. The gruelling way is to have the mother at a distance.

Mavis, Olivia and Dave are forever racing to Wales, Lincolnshire and Derby respectively to look after their distant mother/father. Then they must stay for days or weeks, miles from their chums, work and normal pastimes, making sure that the parent isn't lonely or poorly and have all their shopping, favourite snacks and medicines.

Here, on the other hand, I can just nip up to my mother's garret, give her a quick bowl of gruel, pop on an audio tape, then run downstairs and do as I please: dog walks, cello, homework, visitors. And should my mother topple out of bed, I will hear the crash, be up those stairs like greased lightning, call the emergency services and be hailed as a saviour.

But what will Mavis et al. do should their faraway mothers take a turn for the worse? They must down tools and travel for hours in a panic to be at the bedside, feeling ghastly all the while because they weren't there when it happened and *may now be too late*. I experienced this horror years ago, driving all across town and along stinking motorways, dog and child grizzling in the back of the car, to Hove to visit my ageing parents. Stuck there, I would sit in dreary hospitals and sickrooms for hours, wandering the bleak winter seafront between times.

When Fielding's mother was old and poorly he would trek twenty miles by train and two on foot to visit her on Sundays and wheel her through Chalfont St Peter in all weather – her only outing of the week. On arrival he vowed to be a good son and never argue.

Six hours later, watching the *Antiques Roadshow*, horrid Fielding was arguing like mad with his poor, one-legged mother: about the sugar in her tea or how to draw the curtains, while he knew in his heart that she just didn't want him to leave her. But he was desperate to go, and repaired to the boozer to wash away his guilt. To no avail. He suffered more, but he is still the sinner. I am the saint. Ho ho.

ALL CHANGE

All change at the bloody post office again. First it was change of venue – move to another one because ours was closing. We cannot park outside the new one. But at least we still had our pension books. Sign the book, get the cash, take it home, so my mother could stash the money under her pillow. A simple procedure.

Now all change again. We can't have the book, we must have the card. Easier to lose, but compulsory. Read this letter, ring this number, then we will send you a letter of invitation, say the pension persons, then take the letter to the post office, get a form, fill it in, take it back, they'll give you another form, fill it in, take it back with your passport, memorise your pin number, then you can have your card and money.

I do all this. My mother has managed her wibbly, post-stroke signature, I have remembered the passport, all relevant documents, dog leads and equipment, my purse, Rosemary's yellow peppers that I promised her and my keys. I leave the house with everything I need. What an achievement.

Not good enough. 'This is like a passport form,' says the post office chappie. 'You must write every single letter inside the boxes. They won't accept this.' Because a couple of whiskers of pen stroke were sticking over a box edge, I must go home and do the whole stinking thing again.

I have a scream on the pavement. And in the car. 'Stop it!' shouts Rosemary. 'Will you calm down!'

Oh, ha ha. She is a fine one to talk. The other day she was shouting and tantrumming at her telly over that silly programme about Patricia Amos, who was sent to prison because her daughters had been truanting. A printout page of boxes appeared on Rosemary's TV screen. The boxes containing noughts showed unauthorised absences.

When Mrs Amos was in prison, Rosemary gave her bereavement counselling and pointed out to the court that the Amos family's troubles started when the grandma died. Did anyone pay attention to Rosemary's sensible theory? No. Three years later they are still filling boxes with noughts.

Just a word of advice to our leaders. Minimise those boxes. Otherwise, prepare for a general rise of blood pressure, madness, breakdown and confused elderly persons wandering the streets trying to remember pin numbers. You have been warned.

DISOBEDIENT MOTHERS

Although feeble, speechless and almost completely bedridden, my mother is still defiant. She will not stop feeding the dogs dangerous snacks. Here we have two dogs with delicate stomachs and recurring colitis, but she will stuff them with gingernuts, sweeties, lumps of fat and gristle, cakes and anything that the false teeth cannot demolish.

Time and time again I have begged her not to do it, provided alternative dog snacks on her tray, showed her the vet's bills, described the vile consequences of her actions: the mopping up of vomit, blood and excrement, but will she stop it? No. Down goes the hand with the poisoned snack the minute my back is turned.

Every scrap on her plate may have gone, but down whose throat? I interrogate my mother. 'Did you give them your dinner?' There she sits, a little old lady with pale-blue eyes in pastel bed jacket affecting innocence. She shakes her head in a simpering way. Visitors gaze at her soppily and think her adorabubble. But downstairs the kitchen floor is awash with crap and sick, the garden spattered with puddles of heaven knows what, while my mothers swears blind that not a morsel of lamb chop/Turkish delight/tortilla chips has passed the dogs' lips.

This is a favourite wheeze of mothers and mothers-in-law. It brings them love and adoration from the dog, while simultaneously providing opportunities to defy and enrage their bossy daughters. No wonder Mavis's mother-in-law is forever slipping the dog dicey treats, although she is forbidden to do so. Last week Mavis noticed mother-in-law's hand down by her side, trailing the golden syrup spoon. She is the dog's favourite person in the world, because she drips snacks and sweeties.

For three whole years Andrea begged her mama not to give the dog chocolate, to no avail, until one day, the mama's friend told her about a magazine article warning that chocolate was poisonous for dogs. 'Why didn't you stop me?' she screamed at Andrea, proving that a daughter's place is always in the wrong. Especially if she is in charge.

At least Rosemary's mother only has a stone cat in the garden, but she does have her own little ritual around it. 'We have to decorate it according to the season. Sparkling tinselly collar, little toys, windmills and things,' drones Rosemary. Lucky she. A stone cat has no appetite or bowels.

POPE/CAMILLA

This has been a fearfully difficult week for my mother. Not only is she very poorly, but the telly has been blanket Pope, Charles and Camilla, her three least favourite persons. Day after day we switch on the telly, desperate for a bit of diversion from the daily bore of the sickbed, but it's Pope, Pope, Pope, death and weeping Catholics.

What bad luck, because in our house a) we are atheists and infidels and b) we are trying our best not to think of death. We already have the Reaper at the door turning my mother yellow, and we desperately need a romcom on screen to perk things up. Of course there is a real one going on: the royal wedding, if only my mother could bring herself to have a laugh. What twists and turns: the Queen in a sulk, the church in a bate, the guests being buggered about. Were my mother feeling less weedy, she would be thrilled to bits, but she only gazes at the telly glumly and waves the dreary visions away.

Years ago, when my mother's liver went haywire and she saw spots, we blamed Camilla. Many more forgiving persons have warmed to Camilla, but being in love with the heavenly Diana, the C-word has always thrown my mother into a fury, and fury is bad for the liver. And my mother tends to keep stoking her fury and likes to maintain it at a rolling boil. She is not one for forgiveness, confession and absolution. 'They stick their bums in holy water,' she used to shout rather coarsely, 'and then they go and do it all over again.'

Thank heavens for *Emmerdale* and *Casanova*. A few hours of respite. But the worst is not over. Another sickening vision looms up on the screen: Mr and Mrs Blair in black, mourning the Pope – another weepy face, another veil – two more creatures for my mother's rogues' gallery, and a taster of what is to come: the election and weeks of solid Blair. Rosemary rings to remind me.

'Blair for Pope. He wants the job,' cries Rosemary, slightly maddened by the way the world is going. But as she speaks, the doorbell rings. 'Your auriculas are arriving,' shouts Rosemary excitedly. 'Do you remember? We ordered them months ago. They're black.' Thank you. I am off to the DVD shop to rent some Danny Kaye.

YELLOW

My poor mother almost certainly has liver cancer. She is going yellower by the day, but hanging on grimly. Another friend definitely has cancer and another friend, only my age, has suspected cancer. Cancer everywhere. 'Three out of four get it,' says a nurse breezily. What a fright. Who will be next? Where is it secretly brewing?

We are not mentioning the c-word to my mother. Why bother? She is scared to death of it. Her mother died of it, her brother died of it and her sister died of it, horribly. Why give her a dreadful fright, when we don't officially know? She is too old and weedy to be sent to a hospital for tests, so we all hang about, waiting and wondering.

Meanwhile, the dog has an odd lump on its chest, its friend has a big lump on its gum, Sylvia has an odd stomach ache, I have a strange cough and several hundred moles, some of which sometimes feel peculiar, and then, chilling news, Daughter also spots a tiny lump on her gum.

Every pain or blemish now gives me a fright. I dare not check, because it is usually late at night when I think about checking mole changes or lumps, then what if I find one? I'll have to sweat all night by myself thinking of death and not be able to alert the doctor till morning. But in the morning one doesn't think of these things. Other things are happening.

For a start, my bedroom wall is being painted yellow. It had some blotches and needed redoing. It already was yellow, now it's yellower. But suddenly the yellow doesn't look lovely and sunny any more. It is a nasty message from a fading liver. Why did I not change it when I had the chance?

Then suddenly my mother perks up again. 'What's the matter with me?' she asks.

'Your liver isn't working properly.' And she is also ninety-nine, but I shan't remind her. She requests some ice-cream and ginger sauce. She eats it. She drinks an entire cup of tea. Nothing hurts. She looks better than yesterday, God knows how. Then some marvellous news. Daughter's lump has gone. It was a false alarm, and Olivia reminds me that several more friends have all had cancer, recovered and are still here. But at ninety-nine the outlook is probably not so rosy. More yellow.

DISTRACTIONS

Rosemary and I have discovered a new skill late in life: we can concentrate. Rosemary concentrates on Spanish classes, I concentrate on history classes and cello. Although my playing is still fairly poor, the tone weedy, the notes rarely spot on and the sound of it would drive my poor mother to drink if only she could swallow, how fortunate that I plodded on with it and can play in an orchestra. This is the perfect thing to do when one is trying not to think of catheters, bed sores and a wasted mama. Stop concentrating for two seconds and the Beethoven has galloped away without you.

And if orchestras are not up your street, can I recommend going back to school? If this century stinks, why not plunge into another one? I have plumped for the eighteenth — best music, best jokes. And Rosemary is riveted to her Spanish dictionary. She trots along to her class, she concentrates like mad, but all too soon she must wade back into the morass of her normal life: her unplanted seeds, her unreturned library books, countless hours spent crouching in front of the little clock sign, fiddling and wondering how to stop the central heating and hot water blazing all through summer, and a message written to herself — 'Ring Janet on Friday.' Who the hell is Janet? Which Friday? Has she already rung this person?

But at least, for a short while now and again, we can block out the world. We have suddenly learnt how to brush aside our problems and compartmentalise. Until now I had always thought this an exclusively male skill. But no. Elderly women can do it too. When I was young and in love, I couldn't concentrate for toffee. But now it is a breeze and fabulous escape. No wonder chaps do it at every opportunity.

Sadly Fielding's main distraction is something of a disappointment. 'The brain locks into the logic and aesthetic of footer,' he drones, and blabbers a little hymn of praise to Rooney: his spatial awareness, defiance of gravity, top-spinned, side-spinned and curled balls, and tonight's game is crucial. Or he wallows in rock and roll, or Tommy Cooper videos. 'It's an escape from this crap election and the tragic universe,' he cries dramatically.

Not too tragic. When the sun shines it looks rather charming. My mother doesn't want to leave it. I can see why.

GOODBYE

My mother died two weeks ago. She had wanted to go for years, so she said, but when the time came she didn't seem to fancy it at all. She pretended nothing hurt, refused to take her morphine, defied the doctor's predictions and hung on for two extra weeks, even though life had become horribly grim.

But who can blame her? What a terrifying prospect. And we suspect she had another reason for hanging on until the bitter end. She was still sure we couldn't look after ourselves without her.

Of course Rosemary tried to reassure her that we could manage, but we don't know if she believed it. Aphasia and terminal exhaustion rather put paid to any last words, thoughts, wishes or instructions. We guessed that she vaguely hoped my father was floating around somewhere waiting for her to arrive, but she knew she couldn't count on it. What bliss if one could only believe that a huge bevy of old chums, relatives and long-gone pet dogs would be waiting up there with a Welcome Home notice, but we can't.

Meanwhile the sun is shining, the ravishing tree-peony has come out, so have the lilies of the valley, the roses and for the first time ever, last year's orchids, my mother's absolute favourites, are blooming again. But she is missing the lot. Luckily she's seen them ninety-nine times already, but things would be easier down here if the world didn't look quite so charming.

Then there are the other things that we cannot easily look at: the favourite old woolly, the photos, clothes, little bits and pieces. Daughter has plastered the house with glamorous photos of her grandma: dancing, riding motorbikes and horses, crossing the equator, prancing on a beach with boys, posing on a boat, swimming, cooking, bossing, roaring, laughing – so we don't have to remember

293

the final shrunken little person who wasn't really her at all.

But ninety-nine isn't bad going. I am free to go out. No more commodes, medicines, nappies, false teeth, Zimmers and stairlift. But how odd it is not to have a mother any more, after all this time. I am on the top layer and in sole charge. I notice that my mummy cried out 'Mama' a couple of days before she died. She perhaps thought her mother might be hanging around nearby to help her, but she wasn't. Now neither is mine.

THE ROOM

My mother has gone, but her room is still here, full of her things, which need to be sorted out. What a grim task, and tricky, because how is one to sort out a room if one can't stay in there for more than two minutes without blubbing? In I go, spot the curlers or the ear-rings, and run out again bawling.

The best technique, I find, is to run in, grab a couple of items, or tidy a few inches of dressing table, then run out again, and each time, I stay a bit longer. Chums have offered to do it for us, but do we want them to or not? We can't decide what bits we do or don't want. We want the scrappy old diary, we want the photos, we don't want the spare false teeth. Or do we? A moment of hesitation. No, we don't. Quick. Into the bin.

I suspect it helps to be in a temper. I am in one over the pesky stairlift. It may be fairly unattractive, but it works perfectly, there must be someone out there crawling up and down stairs on their knees who would adore it, but can we give it away? Not a chance. We've tried every organisation going, but they have all spurned it, so we must pay to throw it away. And Rosemary has rejected our sur-plus nappy mountain on her mother's behalf. What luck my mother knows nothing of all this. She would be turning in her urn.

Fielding had terrible difficulty sorting after his mother's death, especially opening her wardrobe. He steeled himself, wrenched it open, stuffed everything into black bin-liners, rushed it to the Oxfam shop, but bad luck, within a week his daddy died as well. Back to the undertaker went Fielding and his brother. 'Same again,' they said, not wanting to be unfair. Then they had another wardrobe to empty.

But some clearing out is not so dreary. I'm weeping in the room over my mother's sepia photos, and come across one of my grandma looking stunningly smart. 'Mummy at my engagement to Leo', my mother had written underneath. Who? How many husbands has my mother had? One called Benny, then my father, and now another surprise one. Is there something I don't know about? And never will? At least I've been sitting in here for twenty whole minutes. Definite progress.

DOG FOOD

How odd it is being free at last. No poorly mother to look after, no Gardener skulking about, hardly any shopping or cooking to do, nothing to rush back home for. But after ten years, one cannot easily kick the habit. I still have a strange longing to stay indoors, or visit the supermarket and cram my trolley with bulk delicacies, bargains and three-for-two of anything going, but what for? To moulder in the larder.

So thank heavens for the dogs. They have saved my bacon. They cannot be left alone for long, they need tons of food, and they have health problems. They are fulfilling all my needs: something to flap over, rush home for, shop for and spend a fortune on. Soon I am resentful, bankrupt, anxious, worn out and happy again.

Now both dogs have a ghastly stomach complaint. They require an exquisitely balanced diet costing half the Royal Mint, plus medicines and fairly constant attention. Meanwhile I am almost penniless and living on baked potatoes and pasta. I go trailing out with my spinster basket on wheels and purchase the odd vegeburger and grains, occasionally splashing out on a tiny morsel of protein, sacrificing myself for the dogs. Bliss.

Fielding is also experiencing freedom. Now he has retired from the horrors of the chalk face, he can doze in his garden under a tree in dappled sunlight. Yesterday he achieved little: broke the coffee pot, watched *Moby Dick* and fell asleep. He does not find his new life a struggle, but it does rather get up Mrs Fielding's nose. There is nothing more enraging than to see someone flopping about relaxing while you are slaving away.

But last week I was forced to mellow out. Some chums invited me to the pub. Daughter was at home, the dogs were not alone, I couldn't dredge up an excuse, so I went out for beer and crisps, a novelty for me. But bad luck, it was footer night – the Liverpool game.

'Could you have been luckier?' shouts Fielding. 'You saw history!'

No, I did not. I saw madness: grown-ups crying, bellowing, jumping about, and a woman who can never bear to watch footer at home and see her children so agitated. But here she could go wild and scream or weep. What a jolly evening, but I left before the penalty shoot-out. I still have some standards.

TEMPER, TEMPER

I used to think that one day, when my mother was no longer here, I would do everything I had no time for when she was alive: write a novel, train the dogs, practise the cello, answer letters promptly, bath regularly, smarten up, mellow out. Wrong as usual. I am still diddling about in the slum. Or falling asleep. The dogs are defiant, the garden a jungle, the bills and scores of lovely condolence letters not answered, the room not sorted out, the cello still scratchy, the novel barely begun, can't be fagged with perfumed baths, and am in a bit of a temper. Because now that I have time, I tend to sit about mulling over Gardener's past misdeeds until my head throbs. A pointless exercise. He is gone, so is my mother, but instead of springing up and functioning, I am fiddling about.

'I told you this would happen,' says Rosemary, the bereavement counsellor, rather bossily. 'You mustn't try to do anything much for a year.' But I defied her and went out to City Hall, that sideways, bollock-shaped building stuck next to the Tower of London. What a dispiriting place. Cross a concrete wasteland, enter the bleak and cavernous entrance area, and a nasty black glassy ceiling hangs in a low and oppressive way over one's head. And my rendezvous was in the basement. Bleaker and bleaker. How everyone managed to stay cheery in the dingy basement of the bollock-building is a tribute to human endurance. I screamed the minute I got out.

'Displacement behaviour,' says Rosemary strictly.

Meanwhile Rosemary hasn't a spare minute; her mother is thankfully still alive, but she also diddles, falls asleep and is pretty foul-tempered. I can't think why. Yesterday she went to visit her mother, taking a map of America that had been requested. But her mama rejected it, because she had already obtained one herself – a

299

Leprosy Foundation balloon, depicting the globe. Rosemary sat on the edge of her mother's bed blowing up the leprosy balloon. Then she had to dash about doing scores of errands, all very particular, seething all the while because she was late for lunch with a chum. And she has another relative who is annoying her intensely. Also still alive. What is Rosemary displacing? Do her theories hold water? Where does time go? Ought I to sit down and think about it? Zzzzzz zzzz . . .

DEATH ROW REVISITED

Rosemary rang last week shouting, 'Switch the telly on.' It was a grisly exposé of goings-on in the geriatric ward of the Royal Sussex Hospital, Brighton. Memories of Hell. Eleven years ago my father died there on a trolley next to the scan machine, which he had finally reached after months of delay. Too late.

Now here is the really grim news. When my parents lived in Hove we used to beg that they be sent to the Royal Sussex. Why? Because the alternative, Brighton General, was even worse. We called it Death Row. Few elderly people, of our acquaintance, came out alive. One day I visited my father there. He was wandering the ward, muddled and covered in shit. His sister, coincidentally, was in the next ward, her bed sodden with wee. With the ward stinking of excrement, in came the lunches. No one helped the half-dead patients to eat them. What century were we in? Soon my father died, sent at last from this miserable pit to his final trolley.

This all explains why I brought my mother here, because she too was sent to Death Row. One parent dead on a trolley is enough for anyone. Curses, curses, that I didn't manage to rescue my poor daddy as well. But on a cheerier note, I recently heard that in his youth, my father, his brother and my grandpa dressed up as gangsters, – Al Capone-style, hats and handkerchiefs across the face, ran into the grumpy brother-in-law's shop and stole the till. Auntie screamed behind the counter, customers fainted, but they dragged the till away, ran off with it and hid round a corner, laughing.

What an amusing fellow my father was, and stunningly handsome, even when old and poorly. Charmed nurses would cluster voluntarily around his bed, but the nurses in Death Row had no time to cluster. I don't like to keep banging on about the dying elderly, but

I notice that they are at last in the news – two programmes on horrid ways of pegging out in one week. Perhaps because the baby boomers have noticed that the Reaper has his eye on us, and we refuse to fade out painfully and nastily in dump hospitals. I never say my prayers, because I have no faith, but now I find myself on automatic, mumbling 'Please God, send the *Panorama* team undercover into Brighton General. At once.'

POST OFFICE

A letter arrives from the post office. It is a statement of my late mother's pension account, which is filling with money. Why? Three months ago I told the pension persons that my mother was dead, would they please stop paying her. Like a good girl, I filled in their form and sent it back with the death certificate. They have taken no notice.

Naturally I ring and ask why. Because, says the spokesperson, I have sent everything to the people who pay the pension, but this lot are the ones who distribute it. So why didn't the post office payers tell the post office distributors my grim news? No answer. Isn't that rather silly? No answer. Do they know their arse from their elbow? No. But they want another death certificate.

As I haven't taken the money, why can't the post office just keep it? Because they can't. I must take it, then I must pay them back. Why? No answer. But to do this I need a deceased account form from the post office, fill it in, enclose relevant documents, take it all back to the post office and they'll send it off.

I go. The post office chappie can't find the deceased account form. Rosemary gets one from her post office. Fill in the form. Use black ink. Do not let one whisker of writing stick out of the boxes. Do not pass go.

I have long suspected a secret plot to drive us all barmy. It's been going on for decades. In 1971 Fielding was unemployed and queueing up for the dole: everyone smoking, human tragedies, people weeping. Fielding was a graduate. Why had he come to this? After several horrible hours, he reached the end of the queue and gave his details 'Wrong queue,' said the woman. 'Join the other one.' Fielding remonstrated to no avail. He left the building, re-entered a labyrinth, found the other queue, more waiting, weeping, smoking, tragedy. At last he reached the end. The same woman was there. Same place, different window. She swivelled her chair round. 'Your details please?'

Clearly nothing changes. But it does, says Rosemary. It gets worse. In Rosemary's post office everyone seems to queue for benefits on Monday mornings only. The queue trails out of the post office, mingles with the bus queue, blocks the pavement, maddens the pedestrians. Big Brother is watching. And laughing.

ASHES

Last week we scattered my mother's ashes, as instructed, on top of my father's ashes, around a rose bush in Brighton. Then, as instructed, we had fish and chips in the beach café and even swam in the sea.

'Look,' said the Daughter, pointing everywhere. 'Grandma used to sit on this wall, that bench, this bit of beach, crossed the road just here.' Ghosts of my parents everywhere. There is my mother on a deck chair, there is my father staggering to the betting shop, there is their beach hut which blew away in the big storm, and here's their flat, and the same darling neighbours upstairs, who have made us a lovely tea and the same lemon meringue pie, in the same-shaped living room.

It is rather charming in Hove: seagulls squawking, smell of the sea, fresh air. But I was often bored stiff coming to stay. And Daughter didn't fancy it once she was a teenager. Now she is older, she wishes she had some grandparents left to visit, but it's too late. And I wish I had done this, that and the other, also too late.

'There's nobody nice here now they've gone. It's no fun any more,' say the old neighbours, making us blub at the tea table.

Back home I have an odd desire to play Bob Dylan, over which I can weep in a maudlin way, thinking of my youth, lost decades ago. But why bother? Youth is often rather grim. I was a prune-faced teenager and thought my parents rather vulgar. When one is sixteen and sensitive, it is tough to have a mummy who speaks very loud French abroad and very loud English everywhere else, and a father who wears pretend donkey's ears when out and about, to show that he works hard. Now I wear the ears myself while at my desk, thinking poignantly of my daddy, but too late again. Why couldn't I have

305

had more of a laugh a decade earlier? Why the piss-face?

This is the trouble with youth; they are a generally scornful lot and tend to think the next generation up a load of old rubbish. To them colourful, outrageous and amusing means loud, shameful and pathetic. Fielding was only ever embarrassed by his mummy. At sixteen he was a learned existentialist. She was more interested in her runner beans. Beans to beans, mothers to ashes.

POO AND FLOWERS

While searching for a new home I notice that all the properties I visit are immaculately tidy: empty sinks, barren desktops and draining boards, beds made, children's toys attractively stacked, no visible newspapers, no crumby breadboard. These dwellings may be pokier than expected with gardens divided into mini-sections –'that's your bit, down at the end, and you also have a quarter-fragment of this patio' – but how tidy and fragrant they are.

How do these people do it? I can't. I have scrubbed, cleansed, tidied, sorted and thrown out tons of crap until I have no other life, but my house is still a dog-scented slum dwelling. And I still have not emptied my mother's room. Now I must, because persons will be coming poking and prying around and the room is chock-full of possessions.

Olivia comes round to help. What a saint, and luckily for me *Gladiator* is on telly. I can do ten minutes in the room, then a chunk of *Gladiator*. Two bags of vests and nighties, ten minutes muscular slaves, fights and blood. Then I foolishly look through a diary. My mother has triumphantly written 'POO' at intervals, to mark the happy days on which she managed to do one. Then ticks for the number of drinks swallowed, then the odd pressed flower – a bit of orchid, a passion flower. By this stage she could no longer manage essays, so she stuck to the POOs in capitals, ticks and flowers, her final interest. I needed twenty minutes of *Gladiators* for the diary, with vicious Emperor, stabbings, plottings and incest.

'Now behind the door,' says Olivia. A difficult area. Coats, hats and dressing gowns. They have hung untouched for months. But not by the stinking moths. They have gobbled up my mother's fur coat and two more favourite coats. Thank heavens she will never know.

307

Meanwhile Russell Crowe has been rewarded for his life's struggle, gone to heaven in his cut-off blouse, and is meeting his stunningly beautiful wife and child in a rural setting with wavy grass. All three are smiling in a dreamy way. If only.

CHRISTMAS ALONE

Here comes my first Christmas alone. No mother, no Gardener, and Daughter will be in sunny Australia. All I need do is toss the dogs a couple of turkey limbs and new squeakies and hide indoors. Could be heaven. I know because I've tried it once, thirty years ago. Sunshine poured through the windows, the sky outside was blue, exquisite music on the radio, perfumed bath, absolute bliss and peace. Then suddenly 'ring ring'. The harpsichord maker called round by surprise. Is there anything more grisly than a surprise visit when one does not want one?

He was carrying a red rose. But it was not for me. It was for the lute-maker woman round the corner who had an enormous bosom, but she was not in. Not only was I fall-back choice, with a relatively insignificant bosom, but my Christmas had been ruined. I had been discovered alone – a tragic figure. What shame. My secret was out. And my bath went cold.

Now I am to have another stab at it. Rejoice. No fighting over size and position of tree, no resentment of seasonal extravagance, no extravagance, no sweltering kitchen, no waves of hatred between family members, no anti-Jesus tantrums by my mother, who was still officially waiting for the son of God to arrive. Just a mellow day with the dogs.

Fielding also longs to be alone, but his family won't allow it. So he understands. 'People rally round, thinking the lonely person might kill themselves,' says he drearily, and Rosemary, out in Argentina, is fearfully jealous of my plan. She was hoping for a lonely lentil bake with me, but the relatives are already gearing up for a grand family Christmas, with multiple wedding videos, charades and carols, and her mother has shingles. She is dredging up all her strength to say

NO. Will she make it? Will she reach the heavenly refuge of my house? I don't mind taking in the odd fugitive.

For ten years my mother rebelled fiercely against Christmas, hoping and praying that each one would be her last. This year her wish has come true. Will mine?